Advance Praise for
Romancing the Holy ...

With great enthusiasm, Debra Farrington
throws open the door to Christian spirituality
and invites all seekers to come in. And a very
wide door it is! Farrington connects with
God, herself, and her community through a
centuries-old discipline like devotional reading
one day and through computer e-mail the next.
Whether on retreat, meeting with her spiritual
director, or participating in a prayer group, she
processes her own experiences to discover the
richness in different approaches to the spiritual
life and — as a true service to newcomers —
offers practical tips on how to get started.
Accessible and encouraging, *Romancing the
Holy* is a wonderful example of the spiritual
practice of hospitality.

— MARY ANN BRUSSAT,
coauthor of *Spiritual Literacy:
Reading the Sacred in Everyday Life*

Romancing
T·H·E H·O·L·Y

Romancing
T·H·E H·O·L·Y

Debra K. Farrington

A Crossroad Book
The Crossroad Publishing Company
New York

1997

The Crossroad Publishing Company
370 Lexington Avenue, New York, NY 10017

All Bible verses are from the New Revised Standard Version.

The cover photo is of a "Shadowcatcher" candle holder available
from Out of the Dreamtime, Inc., 818 Corona Street,
Port Townsend, WA 98368.
Tel.: 800-643-1658.

Printed in the United States of America

Library of Congress Cataloging-in-Publication Data

Farrington, Debra K.
    Romancing the holy / by Debra K. Farrington.
        p.   cm.
    Includes bibliographical references.
    ISBN 0–8245–1648–6 (pbk.)
    1. Spiritual life – Christianity. 2. Spiritual direction.
3. Retreats. 4. Farrington, Debra K.   I. Title.
BV4501.2.F33 1997
248.2–dc21   96–36905
                                                        CIP

To Phyllis and Marcus,
friends, colleagues, and spiritual companions,
who knew about this book
long before I did

Contents

Foreword

I am pleased to write this Foreword to Debra Farrington's new book. A remarkably useful book about the spiritual life, it is simultaneously insightful, personal, and practical.

It takes seriously major changes in the North American religious situation that have occurred over the last half of this century. Two in particular are worth noting.

Until three or four decades ago, being religious was assumed, a virtual given in our culture. In the small Midwestern town in which I grew up in the 1940s and 1950s, everybody I knew — my classmates and their parents — belonged to a church. I didn't know anybody who would say, "Ah, I don't go for that stuff." In a sense, it was still the world of "Christendom," that marriage of Christianity and Western culture which meant that everybody to some degree identified themselves as Christian. Of course, there were regional differences; in some parts of the country, there was a significant Jewish population, as well as a population of nonbelievers. But most people grew up in a religious tradition and took it for granted that they would remain part of that tradition as adults.

That is no longer the case. Among the reasons is a second major factor. Namely, over the same period of time, an older understanding of Christianity ceased to be persuasive to many people. That older understanding was doctrinal, moralistic, exclusivistic, and oriented toward an afterlife. It envisioned being Christian as believing a certain set of teachings to be true and seeking to live in accord with Christianity's ethical teaching (and seeking forgiveness for falling short). It typically affirmed that Christianity was the only way of salvation. And it defined salvation as "afterlife," as going to heaven. Most basically, Christianity was about believing in central Christian teachings *now* for the sake of heaven *later.*

Though this way of understanding Christianity continues to provide a framework for many fundamentalist and conservative Christians, it is no longer compelling to many others. There are millions of people — within the church and the church alumni association, as well as some who have never been part of a church — for whom this older way of being Christian does not work. For these people especially, this book is written.

It takes seriously the growing secularization of consciousness in our culture, which makes many people suspicious of religion as a set of doctrinal claims about the way things are. It also takes seriously our growing awareness of religious pluralism, which makes us suspicious of the claim of any one tradition to be the only way. And it takes seriously the turn to experience which marks the spirituality of many in the modern world: that which I come to know in my own experience can be trusted to be true in a way that that which we learned secondhand from tradition cannot be trusted.

Although this book takes seriously our modern situation, it is also rooted in tradition in the best sense of the word. It introduces the reader to a number of spiritual practices which (with the exception of "spirituality on-line") have been part of the Christian tradition for centuries: spiritual direction, spiritual retreats, prayer groups, spiritual reading, and spiritual community. Each chapter incorporates the author's own experience with broader insights from the tradition and practical guidance for trying out the spiritual practice oneself. Using the metaphor of "on-ramps" to describe these ways of entering the spiritual life, the book itself is an on-ramp.

Almost a century ago, William James in his classic book *The Varieties of Religious Experience* distinguished between firsthand religious experience and secondhand religion. Farrington's book is very helpful for making the transition from believing (or rejecting) secondhand religion to firsthand experience of a relationship with the sacred. It is both an invitation and a guidebook to one's own romance with the sacred.

MARCUS BORG

Acknowledgments

Books do not come into being in isolation, or if they do, this one didn't. My thanks, first, to my editor and publisher, Mike Leach, who came up with the idea for the book and trusted in my ability to put it on paper. He has been a patient, gracious guide and teacher on this journey, which would not have been possible without him.

Thanks go, of course, to friends and colleagues who have offered support and encouragement: Carol Brown, Doree and Ross Laverty, John McAndrew, and the members of my prayer group. And to the bookstore staff, who were generous about the time and demands of the writing process.

My thanks, too, to those who have read all or part of the manuscript and made valuable suggestions: Genevieve Duboscq, Sandy Johnson, and Joe Driskill. Particular thanks go to Kent Gilbert and Mary Ann Brussat for reading, editing, and diagnosing problems — they went above and beyond the call of duty. Thanks also go to many in the Ecunet computer community for their thoughts, their suggestions, and the stories of their journeys. Unending gratitude also to my "Lamaze Class" online (Phyllis Tickle, Mary Ann Brussat, and Sandy Johnson) for keeping me sane over the months of giving birth to this book. And lastly, my thanks to Mark Chimsky, friend and colleague, whose early encouragement of my writing helped more than he knows, who held my hand whenever panic set in, and who gifted this book with the idea for its cover.

Introduction

After many years of managing a religious bookstore, I suppose I have seen just about every kind of person seeking to find a spiritual home. Most recently, a woman who appeared to be in her thirties came into the store looking for one book that would explain the Bible to her. She had grown up in a church, but left it many years ago, and she was toying with the idea of returning. But she felt like she was so far behind in knowing the stories of Christianity that she didn't really dare go to church. I suspect she missed being a part of a religious community, but felt like she needed to pass some "knowledge exam" before she would be welcome there. I applaud her wish to know more of the stories of the Christian faith, but I was sorry that she felt they were a prerequisite for beginning her journey.

Others come into the store looking for books that will open up the world of Christian spirituality for them. Many of these people also left the church years ago, part of the so-called baby boomer generation. Some have experimented with a variety of religions, most particularly ones from the Eastern traditions. Many of them have done this through books, or as a solitary endeavor. And though they have found much of value, they are seeking to go home, in some sense. For many of them, that means returning to the Christian roots that are their own heritage. They are surprised, and pleased, to discover that the spiritual disciplines, and even the deep mysticism of the Eastern traditions, also exist in Christianity. Unfortunately, that knowledge seems to have been kept secret from many in the church over the past decades. But the boomer generation, and others, are seeking to bring these centuries-old traditions back into more common usage.

For me the discovery of these traditions of spirituality has been the key to beginning and deepening my romance with God, with what is holy. That romance began with all the energy and enthusiasm of a new relationship; the discovery of God's presence in my life was a heady one. I quickly learned, however, what most of us learn — that a good, solid relationship takes sustained work and effort over long periods of time.

For me romancing the Holy has meant a reaching out to God, giving time and energy to that relationship. It has been learning that I am worthy of courting God, and of being courted by God. Perhaps hardest of all, for me, it has been about learning to accept God's gifts and presence in my life, learning to believe that I am loved. This romance with God has become a way of life for me now. It is a spiritual way of life.

I write this book for these people, out of my own experience as a baby boomer who is uncomfortable with, yet living within, the church. I believe that there may be something for my generation inside the church, but not all of what is essential about Christianity need be found there. Much of it, if not all, however, is found in Christian community. It is my deepest belief that being a spiritual seeker outside of any kind of community is risky. While much of my meditation and prayer time is done in solitary, it is the guidance and perspective I receive from other seekers that challenges, encourages, and grows me. It is in community that we come to see and learn all the faces of God. Separated always from others, we become isolated, insular, and potentially uncaring about the various communities that surround us.

So where does that leave us? It has been my unearthing and study of the practices found in this book that has sustained me in trying to keep the romance going and growing. I write about them here in hopes that others will discover them as gateways to the beginning of their journeys too. Many people seem to think that going to church on Sunday morning for one hour is the only "on ramp" to Christian life. A Sunday morning service is one on ramp, and it suits some people, but it isn't the only way. The church's history is full of alternative gateways into Christian experience — things like spiritual direction, prayer or spirituality groups, retreats, and spiritual reading. Newer to the religious community, but just as fascinating, is the phenomenon of finding a spiritual community online — over computer networks.

It has always been hard to know what book to suggest to the people who come into the store seeking something that will help them find a starting place on their journey. There are very few books for nonacademics that provide a nontechnical overview of starting places on the Christian journey. This book is intended to help fill that gap, to provide readers with stories and information about possible entry points, or gateways, into Christian community and spirituality.

In the pages that follow, chapter 1 examines the experience of being a part of a church community, the wonderful pieces as well as the more difficult. The remaining chapters in this book explore some of the "gateways" into Christian experience that may be less familiar to you. Each chapter is self-contained, so you can read them in any order that makes sense to you. With stories from my life and others, information on the practices themselves, and suggestions for further reading on the subject, it is my hope that one "on ramp" or another will speak clearly as a pathway for you.

The Church

I hear many stories these days from people who are exiled from their religious traditions.... Many, like me, are members of the baby boom generation who dropped religious observance after high school or college, and are now experiencing an enormous hunger for spiritual grounding. One woman wrote to me to say that she felt a great longing for ritual and community; she said she wanted to mark the year with more than watching trees change. She's joined some political organizations and a women's service club, but found it wasn't enough. She was afraid to even think of joining a church — the Bible makes her angry, more often than not — but she thought she might have to.

—Kathleen Norris, *Cloister Walk*

In my line of work, managing a theological bookstore, I see lots of folks who are searching. They're not always sure what they are searching for. Many are timid or shy with their questions, but their comments betray a deep longing for a spiritual home. They come to the store looking for just the right book, a book that will speak to their hearts, will help them make sense of their world, the book that will fill some deep void in their lives.

I remember being one of those people about fifteen years ago. I discovered a small book by Henri Nouwen called *The Genesee Diary*. I had no idea what I was buying. Like most people who are reexploring Christianity as an adult, I didn't want to ask for any assistance at the store. I wasn't sure if I even really wanted to associate myself with the church again. In fact, I probably couldn't have told you what brought me to the small Christian bookstore on Telegraph Avenue in Berkeley that day. But Nouwen's book turned out to be a very special book. It is his diary of a seven-month retreat with the Trappist monks at Genesee, and it is full of his honest struggles and successes in his relationship with God, with the world, with silence. He talks about anger and rejection, as well as ecstasy and moments of close contact with God. The honesty, and Nouwen's admission of the full range of emotions in connection with his spiritual searching, captured me, and I began to give more serious thought to rediscovering my own Christian background. I still have that small volume, signed now by Nouwen, and over the years, I have suggested it to many of those who have come to the store seeking a special book.

Books are wonderful things, and excellent companions for the journey. If I didn't think this was true, I would not have been a bookseller for the last twenty years. Nonetheless, books can help us in our spiritual journeys only up to a point. Books can open doors for us. They can provide all sorts of much needed information and opinion. They can become time-honored friends that we return to often. But the religious journey is not primarily a book journey. It is not a completely solitary endeavor. Even many of the men and women who went off into the desert in our early Christian history spent years in Christian community before going off into solitary places with God.

The religious journey, and most particularly for the purposes of this book, the Christian journey, is a community endeavor. We can read, pray, and study in solitude sometimes — even often. But we miss out on something valuable, and we fail to see the full face of God, when we choose to search, all alone, for God. We miss being refined by the love and support, and even the fire and the anger, of the community, a community made up of the various faces and facets of God.

It has taken me many years to learn this, and, to be truthful, I am still working on learning the full truth of these statements. I came back to the church because I felt a large void in my life, one that I hoped the church would help fill. In some important ways, the void has been filled. At the same time, I have spent as much time being annoyed at the church as I have being thrilled with it. I have spent as much time wanting to educate those within the church as I have being educated by them. I have railed against policies in the church which seem hypocritical or mean-spirited, but I have also found moments of powerful connection to God through the eyes and experiences of those I meet in church. I struggle to make myself get up and go to church many Sundays, but I am just as unwilling to walk away from the church altogether. I am like the woman in the quote at the beginning of this chapter. I long for the ritual and the community. I long to talk about my journey with others. The church is not always an ideal place for these things, but when it is at its best, it is an unbeatable Christian experience.

I have met many people who would like to reconnect with a Christian community as an adult. Many don't realize that churches aren't the only place to find Christian community, and later chapters of this book suggest other pathways into community. But churches are the most obvious of the Christian communities, perhaps the easiest to find. Many people have memories of church as a child and will want to start reexploring Christian spirituality in church. I understand that longing for the church of our early childhood. It was the starting place for me too.

I was born in Schenectady, N.Y., in September of 1955 to a mother and father who were Methodist and American Baptist, respectively. Mom was a PK — parson's kid — with a father who was a Methodist minister, one who had served as a missionary in China for a while. It was my grandfather who baptized me as an infant. My great-grandfather, too, was a Methodist minister and bishop. Dad's family was American Baptist, the more liberal wing of the Baptist Church.

My earliest memory of anything religious comes from my very youngest years, a fuzzy memory of a circle of people at a Unitarian church in upstate New York, where we'd moved when I was very young and where I grew up. I was probably no more than two years old. I have no idea why we — adults and children — were all in a circle, but I remember the room being sunny and bright, and the memory has a strong and positive feel to it. My parents, new in town, went to the Unitarian church because they knew other people who attended there, but our time in that church was short-lived. My dad, though he had his doubts and questions about traditional Christian theology, found the Unitarian church to be less satisfying than his traditional Christian faith. While I was still very young, we transferred to the Presbyterian church in town.

The Presbyterian church was a big stone building,

like many old Eastern churches, situated on a corner
in what was then a lively downtown area. In my memory, I remember the church as being busy, always full of
people. I remember the sanctuary as a very dark place,
with little natural light, but dark in a warm and comforting sort of way. What natural light there was in the
sanctuary came filtered through colored stained glass
windows, which contributed to the sense of quiet and
comfort within.

I have some vague memories of Sunday school, of
bright spaces filled with pictures of Bible stories and
characters on the walls. Unlike my memories of the
quiet sanctuary, my memories of Sunday school are
noisy memories. We must have learned many of the
Bible stories children learn in Sunday school, as I don't
remember a time anymore when I didn't know the basic stories. In them, God was always pictured as an
old white man, with white hair and beard, sitting on
a throne "up there" somewhere, looking down on us.
There was also a portrait of Jesus on the walls. The
painting was probably a standard portrait in the 1950s,
a white Jesus with long hair, staring slightly upward,
with a look of deep longing on his face. It would take
another twenty-five years for me to discover that Jesus,
as someone from the Middle East, was not a Caucasian,
and that there were many more and richer images for
God than the man on the throne.

I suspect we sang a lot in Sunday school — I'm sure I

learned the song "Jesus Loves Me" there. And I remember that I was always dressed up, in a fancy dress with my favorite black patent leather shoes. One did not go to church in casual clothing!

During the years we were Presbyterian, my mother's family would often gather for holidays, particularly Thanksgiving and Christmas, and, though family problems would mar later holidays, at least as a very young child, those were happy times for me. The house would be full of people, or we would go to my maternal grandparents' house, which was equally full and noisy. In the midst of it all, however, sat my grandfather, the Methodist minister, quiet and still. In retrospect, I don't know if he was just ignoring the chaos that went on around him, or if his stillness came out of a center that was deeply connected to God. Whatever it was, it impressed me, and I hold a strong memory of it to this day.

My mother, however, was something of a religious pilgrim. Around the time I was ten, she convinced the family to convert to Reformed Judaism, much to the displeasure of my grandparents. Many of my religious memories come from those years. Some, though not all, of the memories of those years are quite pleasant. The time definitely shaped what would be important to me later.

I fell in love with the music of the temple — with chanting in the service, and with the haunting melodies and harmonies of the music. My mother, a good musician, directed the choir, and I sang in it, a natural outgrowth of the musical training I'd received even before I started reading. So much of my life, in fact, was focused on music, even at that young age, that music became, and remains, one of the ways in which I experience God's presence most intensely.

Aside from the music, I learned to treasure the power of ritual in Jewish life, and still carry with me its power to bring order and meaning to my life. The repetition of various rituals, both at home and at temple, week after week, lent stability and predictability to life. I loved the Friday night ceremony of lighting the candles over the Sabbath dinner. Even now, many years later, I can still recite the Hebrew blessing for the lighting of the Sabbath candles. To this day I miss the phrase "Shabat Shalom" and have never found anything in the Christian church which conveys the peacefulness and blessing of Sabbath days inherent in that Sabbath prayer and greeting.

The rabbi of the temple was also a hero for me back then. He was young and good-looking, and I probably had a crush on him. But he was also the one who trained me in the traditions of the temple and took me through my Bat Mitzvah when I was thirteen. I was fiercely devoted to him. But he turned out to be too liberal for the congregation and was forced out not long after my Bat Mitzvah. With his departure, I lost some of my own enthusiasm for the temple, and for the politics of organized religion. It was my first, though certainly not my last, exposure to politics within a religious institution, and it left a bad taste in my mouth even then. And though there were many things I loved, and still treasure, about the years I was Jewish, I never really felt like an insider. Many of the Jewish children my age taunted me about not being "really Jewish," and I suppose they were right.

The 1960s were in full swing by that time, and affected me deeply. I'd been educated, through sixth grade, in the state university's experimental school, which aside from teaching academic subjects, taught me to think independently and experientially. Though I wasn't a trouble-maker, per se, I wasn't very fond of authority, and I felt little or no loyalty at all toward institutions. These were the years too, in which my parents divorced, a time of great confusion and chaos for me — chaos and confusion for which the temple had no answers, only disdain. Feeling angry about the treatment of the rabbi, and feeling like an outsider anyway, I left the temple, and all organized religion, somewhere around age fourteen.

I tell this story, not because it is unique, but because it is not particularly unusual. Though most of us who grew up in the so-called baby boomer generation didn't get exposed to multiple religions as I did, many of us got religious training of some sort as a child, but bolted from the church as soon as we were given an option to do so. For many of us, that was sometime in high school or when we went away to college.

We all had different reasons for leaving. I left because of political intrigues and my own liberal leanings, which were not welcome in the temple. Others left for the simple reason that the church was something their parents did, and they tried very hard to avoid being like their parents. Church wasn't "relevant," and being relevant was all-important. I have talked to others who left because they were gay or lesbian and, hence, felt unwelcome. Others felt actively betrayed by the church or its staff or volunteers in a variety of ways. Many religious institutions are only now beginning to acknowledge some of the damage done to parishioners by priests, pastors, and others in positions of authority. There were many reasons why we left the church, but the bottom line is that we left, and we left in large numbers. Growing up in the 1960s and 1970s, we had better things to do than worry about the institutional church.

❦

Once I'd left the temple, I doubt that I thought much about religion during the remainder of high school or during my college years. I certainly don't remember attending a service of any sort during those years, or having many friends who attended a temple or church.

In high school, I spent my time with a small crowd of students, many of us with parents connected to the local state university. We considered ourselves the "intellectuals" around school and shunned events like football games and proms in favor of "hanging out" at the home of one of our crowd, playing guitars, going to drive-in movies, having parties. Following high school, I went to a women's college in southern California and got a B.A. in American Studies.

After college, I moved to northern California, and got a job in Berkeley managing the textbook department of the bookstore at UC Berkeley. Those were busy career years for me, and my work took up all of my time and attention. The job took me traveling a good bit and proved challenging on many fronts on an almost continual basis. I was teaching classes and training seminars of various sorts, working with booksellers and publishers around the country. I even experimented with academia for two years and got a master's degree in folklore while at UC Berkeley, doing the degree work full-time on top of my job. The pace of life was nonstop, focused almost solely on career goals.

Suddenly, however, at age twenty-nine, I began to absolutely dread turning thirty. Though I understood intellectually that it wasn't rational, I was convinced that I would wake up on my thirtieth birthday as an old woman, with none of my body parts functioning well, my life essentially over. I began to sense that I had put too much of my life on hold, that I was waiting for who-knew-what, and that at age thirty I was not doing many of the things I wanted to do in this life. Even though I was incredibly busy, my life suddenly felt empty.

At about the same time, one of my sisters, who had also dropped out of organized religion as a teenager, began talking with enthusiasm about the Presbyterian church she had recently begun attending. I was aware, too, that a friend and colleague in the bookstore attended a church she enjoyed. She talked about it occasionally and seemed to spend a lot of time there. I must have sensed that perhaps the church held something I needed at that point. One day, I asked my bookstore colleague if I could go to church with her that following Sunday. She just about fell off her chair in surprise, but she was glad to take me along with her.

The church she took me to was a liberal Protestant (United Church of Christ) church. My friend introduced me around, and I quickly became a regular at the church. Over the next few years I grew enormously in that church environment. It became the strong and stable place that held me as I began to explore some of the more painful memories of my childhood. It was a place where I began to question my childhood understandings of God and to develop new, more mature ones. I remember one particularly powerful conversation with the senior pastor at that time. I'd gone to him to ask why we had to hear so much about sin every Sunday in church. It seemed like we talked about sin endlessly, and that began to feel heavy beyond bearing. His question to me — "Why are you hearing us talk about sin so much when we are talking about love as much or more?" — opened all sorts of doors to my spiritual life and understanding. I began to see that I believed in a God who considered me "not good enough" rather than a God who "loved me, no matter what." My own vision of a judgmental God, rather than a loving God, predisposed me to hear harshness in the Sunday morning service.

This same minister taught a twelve-week class in the church in which a group of about twenty of us explored methods of prayer from an experiential standpoint. It was one of the great formative experiences of my life, as well as one of the most intense. Each week in class we were exposed to some new spiritual practice. One week, for instance, we read the New Testament parable about the Prodigal Son (Luke 15:11–32) and were asked to imagine ourselves as one of the characters of the story and write our own version of it. In the parable, one son asks his father for his inheritance, squanders it, and then returns home to a father who is immensely pleased to have him there. The son's older brother, however, is livid and cannot understand why the father celebrates the reappearance of the younger son rather than his own steadfast service to his father. I found myself identifying with the older son, partly, perhaps, because I am the oldest of four children. I experienced tremendous anger that night as I wrote from the perspective of the wronged oldest child.

On another evening we learned about Quaker dialogues. In these, a question is posed to a group, and silence reigns until someone begins with an answer to the question. From there, each person in the circle answers the question in turn, with no arguments, no responding to others' answers. Usually when others speak, we are formulating our response to their words while they are talking. We are only partially listening to the rest of their words while we work on evaluating what they have already said. I learned the power of just listening to others that night, having been freed from the responsibility of thinking critically about what they were saying.

Perhaps the most powerful and most difficult part of the class, however, was being paired with a different person each week. We were asked to discuss the week's readings together, or to meet and do some particular exercise. It was incredibly awkward, at first, to talk about my spiritual life with others in the group, particularly when I hadn't picked my partner and had gotten someone I wouldn't normally talk with about these things. I felt awkward, too, because at that point in time talking about God in polite company wasn't really done much. It was a new language for me, a language colored with images that made me nervous. Nonetheless, some of those conversations were powerful ones, the awkwardness giving way to some very rich and important words.

I also became a youth leader in that church, working with the large high school group, which was one of my greatest sources of joy for several years. The director of the youth program, a wise and delightful woman, created a rich program which fed the lives of the leaders of the groups as much as it nourished the youth of the parish. While many church youth programs are about activities, this program focused on emotional and spiritual growth, as well as creating community. Our Sunday evenings together were great fun, but they were also times of intense conversation and exploration of important issues in the lives of teens. I became close to some of the kids, as did all the leaders, and took great joy in watching them grow, in being available to them when they needed me. I was also close with many of the leaders, so in many ways, the work with the youth group became the place where I felt most at home in the parish. The group became my small group within the larger church community.

For several years, until I moved to New York for a new job, this church was a strong home for me. I was active there in many ways, working on committees, working with the youth, as well as being involved with the young adult fellowship group. It was certainly not perfect, and I was not without my frustrations there, but it did help me explore my relationship with God, and it helped to fill the void that my busy career could never fill.

When I was a child, I spoke like a child, I thought like a child; when I became an adult, I put an end to childish ways.

— 1 Corinthians 13:11

It has been about twelve or thirteen years since I came back to the church, after an absence of about fourteen years. I came back to find something that would help fill the emptiness I found in my soul, and, as I have said, the church fills some of that. At the same time, by coming back to the church as an adult, I have seen things that I did not see, or did not see clearly, as a child. The church is a human institution, always struggling to hear and follow God's call. As with anything human, some days the church does a better job of hearing God's call than others. It is impossible for me, and for many others I know, to view the church through rose-colored glasses. Nor are we asked to do that, in my opinion. Part of coming back to the church as an adult is to come bringing our ambivalence with us, letting it be an instrument of learning and growth for ourselves and for others.

Those of us who come back to church to explore our relationship with God and one another in prayer often explore Sunday morning worship as a place to do that. We find a wide variety of worship experiences in various churches. When worship is done well, the clergy and congregation seem filled with the presence of God. The words of worship and the prayers (called the liturgy in many churches) are spoken with feeling, with the knowledge that the words speak of profound truths. Hymns are sung with vigor and enthusiasm, and perhaps people find themselves swaying or responding bodily to the music. Even periods of silent prayer can be charged with energy, with the sure knowledge of God's presence. None of this has much to do with the denomination of the church, or the particular style of worship. When people expect God in worship, and when God feels present, worship is a powerful community experience, a thankful response to God's presence in our lives.

Unfortunately, worship is not like this in all churches. Worship is sometimes seen as an obligation, something that takes place in one specific hour each week, and great annoyance breaks out when worship extends past that hour by so much as ten minutes. The words of the liturgy, and the prayers, are read without emotion, without the sense that the words matter, that God hears. Sermons are dry, intellectual exercises rather than words that speak to people's hearts and souls. Hymns are played slowly and mournfully, and the singing is lifeless.

Many exploring church membership will also struggle with issues of inclusiveness in Christianity. It often seems that churches were made for the "typical" family, with two parents, two children, a dog, and a one-family house. For those who fall outside of those parameters — and that includes many people — the church can be a place of alienation. Those of us who are single, by choice or by circumstance, may feel unwelcome to attend an all-church retreat which is called "Family Camp." I remember one particularly painful moment where it was suggested that we call our young adult fellowship group "Pairs and Spares." As a single adult, I do not consider myself a spare, but I often sense that many in the church, consciously or unconsciously, view us that way.

For those who are gay or lesbian, the church can also be a difficult environment. Depending on the denomination, and often on the particular church itself, gays and lesbians find various degrees of welcome. Some churches will gladly welcome gays and lesbians in all facets of church life, while others exclude them from all but marginal participation. Many denominations are currently struggling with the roles they will allow gay and lesbian people to assume within congregations and denominations. Painful battles rage over whether they can be ordained into clergy positions, serve in lay leadership roles, and participate in the full life of the institutional church.

Another of the most divisive issues in many churches today is the question of inclusive language. The words used in worship, in the Bible, and in our culture at large have tended to be exclusively male words, when words that include men and women might seem more appropriate. Many in the church struggle with images of God that seem to be predominantly male, images that do not include the feminine. In some churches, this language reflects the reality of the struggle women must still make if they wish to fully exercise their gifts. Some churches have responded more readily to women's concerns than others. In the more liberal churches that have a different liturgy each week, many have changed the language, making it gender sensitive, or incorporating male and female images of God. In churches where the liturgy is set by the denomination, change comes in other ways. Until the revision of prayer books and worship resources, the language remains the same. Many of us in the pews have solved the problem for ourselves, substituting words and phrases that more clearly convey our own understandings of God.

Many in churches are also asking questions about Jesus these days. When I was a child, we were told that the stories in the Bible were true stories. Period.

Many adults in the church question that understanding today. The publicity of groups like the Jesus Seminar, a group of scholars who are trying to uncover what they can of the actual historical Jesus, has opened the door to questioning. For some of us, the work of people like Marcus Borg, John Dominic Crossan, John Shelby Spong, Robert Funk, and others has given us the possibility of new and stronger faith. They have shown us that not all the stories in the Bible are factually true, that they contain the political and social interpretations of those who recorded the stories. Nonetheless, the stories can and do contain Truth, even if not historical veracity. To be in church, however, is often to be told differently, either in the liturgy or in the sermon, and I still struggle with this many days.

Many, if not all, of these problems existed in the church of our childhood. In all likelihood, we left the church because of some of these concerns. So why come back and deal with them again? Why place ourselves in situations that seem certain to make us angry and frustrated sometimes? For some, going back to church makes no sense. The answers to the questions above are negative answers. Being a church member is not the only way to be a part of Christian community, and it will not be right for everyone. For others, the church community feels unequivocally like home. Most of us, however, will fall somewhere between those two extremes, and find ourselves in an ambivalent relationship with the church, in a relationship that challenges us, and the church, to grow and change.

For me, the reason to consider church membership has to do with the dangers of being a seeker along solitary paths. Though I spend a fair amount of time in solitary prayer and meditation, I need the community of other seekers if I am to truly grow. Left to my own devices, I move further and further inward until, finally, there are no road markers to tell me where I am. I get stuck, and either fail to understand what is happening in my relationship with God, or get endlessly confused about which way to go next. I need the guidance of those who have walked these paths before me, and, at the same time, I need to be a pointer for those who have yet to walk the paths I have walked. I need to see as much of the full face of God as possible. When I seek God on my own, I see only the faces that make sense to me, that are familiar and comfortable. I can ignore anything which does not seem to fit, or which causes me frustration or pain.

For me, the corporate worship experience is what draws me back to the church and keeps me there. I have wandered through a variety of churches in the last nine or ten years, spending time in United Church of Christ, Presbyterian, Unitarian, and Episcopal churches, looking for "the perfect worship service." I have found things that I loved and things that seem meaningless to me in all of those environments. At the base, however, worship is a powerful communal experience of God's presence — God's care and concern, as well as God's challenge — that is not available when one prays alone.

Sometimes that is achieved by participating in powerful rituals. In a Unitarian church in Syracuse, N.Y., that I attended for a while, it was the congregation's tradition to observe All Saints' Day in a deeply touching way. When we came to church that morning, we were invited to take some leaves, made of construction paper, and write on them the names of loved ones who had died. When we entered the sanctuary, there was a large white, naked, tree set up near the altar. About midway through the service, we went up to the tree, row by row, and hung our leaves on the tree, bringing it back to life. Watching that stark white empty tree fill with colorful leaves, each leaf representing the name of a valued loved one, filled me with awe. The sanctuary was suddenly filled with the spirits of those who had died, and with our own remembrances of them. The tree was left in the sanctuary for many weeks, a powerful reminder to us of the communion of all saints, dead and alive.

For many of us in Christian churches, power and comfort can be found in the act of communion, the ritual act of taking bread and wine in remembrance of Jesus' words and life. In its larger sense, it is the communion of all God's people with God. In many churches, it is a time of recollection and a time of individual and corporate communion with God. Communion, or the Eucharist, as it is sometimes called, is administered differently within various congregations and denominations. But in some way or another, bread and wine are served to those who are present, bread and wine that symbolically nourish each individual, and the congregation as a whole, to continue to do God's work in this world. For me, and for many others, communion is an essential part of the worship experience, a time of deep prayerfulness, of acceptance of God's gifts to me, and a time of joyful recommitment to God on my part.

While community ritual is one way God's presence is expressed in worship, the community itself often becomes the presence of God for us. The support and encouragement of a community of like-minded seekers, the sense of the whole rejoicing or mourning with individual members, sustains us and grows us into fuller understandings of God. It is difficult to describe the power of this to those who have not experienced it, but it is that for which many people outside the church seem to long. There is little to equal the thrill of a couple bringing their two-week-old baby to church for the first time on Christmas Eve, or the sadness of a congregation gathered to celebrate and mourn the loss of a member of the congregation. Churches can be filled with people who speak their prayer requests openly during worship services, or through other channels in the church, knowing that they will be held in prayer by the whole. They can be places of laughter, of profound corporate silence and listening, and places where tears of pain are welcome.

Church is about the community of seekers outside of worship as well, and it is often in committees, small groups, or fellowship groups that much of the church's community life takes place. My own experience for many years with the youth group, which provided me with a small community within the church that was a place of support and nourishment to me, is an example of this. It provided me with a group of people that I knew more intimately, with youth who valued my guidance on their journey, and with people who taught me a great deal about living in community and about God.

So, while the church drives me crazy some days, it continues to be a place of challenge and growth for me, and for many others. It keeps me focused on the larger picture in this life, reminds me of the struggles of others, and presents me with opportunities to stretch and learn. It is by being in community that we begin to see our place in the whole of life, that we see the whole face of God. That is the reason that, despite my own frustrations with the institutional church, I stay attached, albeit at marginal levels sometimes. God lives in the church community, even on the days when that seems most improbable.

I am not one who believes that the institutional church is for everyone, but for some people it may, indeed, be a good gateway into Christian life. If you've been away from the church for a long time, however, finding a church home that is right for you can feel pretty intimidating. Perhaps the best place to start is by considering what you hope to find in a church. Things you might consider include the following:

Size of the community: Churches of different sizes have different advantages and disadvantages. Small communities tend to be more intimate environments where everyone knows everyone. It is hard to be anonymous in a small community, even as a visitor. In small churches, the financial and human resources can be somewhat limited, so whatever programming and fellowship that happens is more likely to be intergenerational. In larger churches, it is possible to go unnoticed more easily. Obviously, that is an advantage to some and a disadvantage to others. Because large churches tend to have multiple staff and pastors, more programming is usually offered outside of worship. Many large churches these days are focusing on offering parishioners a sense of closer community through a variety of small-group experiences. This is particularly true of the really large churches, or the so-called megachurches, which usually boast membership in the thousands. Finally, lots of churches fall in the middle range in terms of membership. Medium-size churches offer an eclectic combination of the advantages of both the small and the larger churches.

Location: This matters more to some than to others. In times past, churches were neighborhood or community churches. These days, people tend to shop for churches, finding one that fits their needs regardless of location. Depending on the size of your community, however, church location will, to some extent, govern the type of people it attracts and that you will meet there. Neighborhood community churches without parking lots will attract mostly folks from the immediate area. Large megachurches in suburbs, with acres of parking lots, will attract a crowd from a wide geographical area. If you and/or your family are hoping to become active in a church, perhaps attending evening classes or sending children to youth programs, you may want to consider how far you are willing to drive to attend those programs.

Programming: It is important to consider your needs for fellowship and Christian education as you look for a good church home. Would you like to sing in a church choir? Do you want youth programs for your children? Are you looking for a church that offers courses in prayer and spiritual development? Are you looking for fellowship groups that include other singles, other couples, or other people your age? Do you want opportunities to participate in social justice or community outreach projects through your church?

Worship: Do you have any sense of what kind of experience you want in worship? Is music important to you? Do you prefer an active worship style, or are you seeking a more contemplative worship experience? Do you want lots of ritual, or a minimum of it? Is there something from your own early experiences of church that you would like to find again, or something that you are trying to avoid? Some churches have a worship service in which the words and prayers are different each Sunday, written or assembled by the pastor or a worship team. Other churches have a set worship service that varies little or not at all from week to week. Does one of these appeal more than the other?

Theology: Various churches, even churches within the same denomination (e.g., Lutheran, Presbyterian), tend to focus on certain understandings or directions more than others. Some focus on clearer understandings of the Bible, while another might emphasize social justice issues. Others will center their work on developing Christian community or on developing the prayer and spiritual lives of their members. Various church communities also practice varying degrees of inclusiveness with regard to women, gays, and lesbians. Finally, churches have varying requirements of members to believe in certain ways; some churches welcome questions and debate, while others find certain understandings to be definitive.

Once you have determined what seems to be most important to you in a church home, visiting a variety of churches is the best way to find one that suits you. Looking in the yellow pages of the phone book can provide you with some clues. Increasingly, individual churches and some denominations are posting information about themselves on the World Wide Web, and this can be a useful resource for those with access. You might also ask any friends who attend church about their experiences and their suggestions. But in the end, plan to spend some months visiting churches during their Sunday morning worship services. Attending services and picking up brochures about the church and its activities, talking with other members during a coffee hour that proceeds or follows the worship service, are the best ways to gather the information you need. For those churches that seem of interest to you, ask to be added to any mailing lists for church newsletters, or make an appointment to visit with the pastor and learn more about the church.

Finding and joining or attending a church that feels like a good Christian community for you is one of the ways to begin exploring Christian life and spirituality. For a variety of reasons, it will not be right for everyone, or it may not be right for you at this moment. However, church, or Sunday morning worship, is not the only gateway or path into Christian life. The remaining chapters in this book suggest other starting places for your Christian journey that may work better for you at this time.

– T W O –

Spiritual Direction

Spiritual director — what a wonderful sound that has. Someone to give my spiritual life direction — clear, simple direction. Someone to give me the answers, to tell me how to pray, what to pray. Someone who knows just the right practice that will help me know God intimately and completely, and make my life whole and meaningful.[1]

I think that is what I hoped for when I first entered spiritual direction, and perhaps that's why things didn't ever really work as well as they might have with my first spiritual director. Tom was one of the pastors at a large church I attended in my late twenties and early

---

1. There is much controversy over the term "spiritual director" these days. Most directors, in fact, find the term misleading and inadequate. It gives the impression like my own to many — that the director actually directs and solves problems. Or, as Margaret Guenther writes in *Holy Listening* (Boston: Cowley Publications, 1992), it conjures up "the image of a clerical Svengali compelling a trembling soul to kneel on broken glass while reciting the Miserere" (1). Nonetheless, no one has come up with a better name for the task at this time.

thirties, and one of his main tasks was to help the members of the congregation with the development of our spiritual lives. In and among the programs he ran for groups within the congregation, he also offered spiritual direction to individuals who wished it. So I began seeing him once or twice a month, spilling out stories of my past and my wishes for a different present.

I think I believed that Tom could "fix" everything for me, that he would give me exercises or perspectives that would magically and instantly make everything right. Of course, he couldn't. And that was always vaguely disappointing. Tom was clearly a spirit-filled man, one of those amazing people who appears to be deeply grounded and in whom God shines forth clearly without much of a filter. He was usually very present to people, quiet, calm, and attentive. He seemed to be at peace with the world. I wanted what he had, and perhaps I will have it someday. But from Tom I learned that finding that quiet inner core is a long, slow process, and one that varies tremendously from individual to individual.

Though there were a few years between Tom and my next spiritual director, I don't think I ever gave up wanting to find that quiet inner place — that place where I feel God's presence and feel at one with the world. Life for me as a child and young adult had been chaotic, not without its charms, but not without a reasonable amount of pain from growing up in a family that had been deeply wounded for generations. By the time I was in my late twenties, my primary sense of my world was one of brokenness and sadness, leaning toward depression sometimes. Psychotherapy had been helpful, but only up to a point. There was a nagging sense within me that therapy could take me only so far, and then a leap of faith would be required. Therapy told me some of the sources of my anger and pain, but it could not help me understand the reasons that I had had to suffer. It could not tell me whether God intended that pain for me. In fact, most therapists generally resist discussing such things. So I was left with some sense of healing from childhood difficulties, but thousands of questions about why. Without knowing the "whys" of my life — without knowing if there was a God who intended that I suffer — without a sense of a loving God, a God who *did not* intend my suffering — I could not finally heal.[2]

Linda, my second spiritual director, taught classes at the seminaries where I work. One of the great travesties of many seminaries today is that they offer very little

---

2. Many people confuse spiritual direction and therapy, but their end goals are actually quite different. Therapists work with clients to help them understand the source of their anxieties or problems, and then seek to either resolve the problem or help the client respond to the problem in a healthier fashion. A spiritual director, on the other hand, may work with the same raw material, but his or her focus is on helping the client find God's hand or wishes in the client's life, rather than on resolving the problem per se. The distinction is a fine one but important nonetheless.

spiritual development to the people they are preparing
for the ordained ministry. In many Protestant seminaries, students preparing for the ministry might take
one class in spirituality, often leaving pastors feeling ill-
prepared to deal with people's spiritual crises. So when
Linda taught her classes on spiritual life and disciplines,
she had a class four times the size of most other classes
at the seminaries. Even if she hadn't been one of the
few teaching spirituality, Linda's gentle presence, her
emphasis on healing our wounds, spoke volumes to
the students enrolled in her courses. Over the semester,
Linda spoke to us of prayer and healing weekly, ending
each class with a half hour guided meditation, one of
her specialties.

Linda invited each student to come to her office once
during the course of the semester to discuss with her
any issues, concerns, or feelings that arose for us out
of the material and meditations presented in class. I
don't remember any of the specifics of our conversation that day, but I remember feeling hungry to have
a place to discuss my spiritual life on a regular basis. I
had discovered, by that time, that churches were often
a poor place for these conversations, that discussions
of one's spiritual life and practices made many church
folks squirm. There were not many other places to discuss spiritual understandings in my world either. After
thinking about it for a couple of weeks, I got up the
courage to ask Linda if she would be my spiritual di-

rector and was delighted (and a little scared) when she agreed.

❧

Many of those who write about spiritual direction today report that the use of spiritual directors is on the rise in the last decade or so. Seeing a director seems to have touched a deep chord within this generation, giving people a previously unavailable place to discuss matters of spirituality. Various individuals seek out spiritual direction for a variety of reasons. What I have heard most often from those who have sought direction is that they seek someone who, as one friend put it, knows God better than we do. They seek someone who has deliberately sought out God's presence and wisdom, who seems to be further down the path than they are, someone who can act as a guide and mentor on the journey.

Many people seek out a guide with an expertise they feel they lack. For many of us, our knowledge of Christian faith is limited to a few statements we learned or heard as children, statements which are inadequate for us as adults. We seek out someone who can guide us into a fuller knowledge of a faithful life, who can help us find answers to our questions about Christian spirituality and theology. Often people come with basic and important questions like: "What is prayer and how do I do it?" and "Who or what is God and what does God intend for me?" They come hoping to find out how to live a fuller, more deeply connected and faithful life.

Others come to spiritual direction without knowing quite why they come. They seek the meaning of life, as they discover that work is not the most important focus of their lives. They come with disturbing dreams that tell them something is wrong, but they don't know what. Some come, as I did, because self-help books and therapy are just not quite enough to help us heal.

We seek out spiritual direction using a variety of words and reasons: healing, training, knowledge, encouragement, a safe place to talk. Fundamentally, however, we seek out someone who knows more than we do. Like a novice seeking a teacher, many of us eventually find that our own resources are not enough and that a guide is needed. We need someone who has been further along the path than we have been, someone "who knows God better" than we do, because at the deepest level, whether we know it or not, what we really seek is God. We need to know God, to know that we are loved — unconditionally — by God. Once we come to understand that, we can find the things we thought we sought: healing, peacefulness, knowledge of ourselves, connectedness to our world. That is the work of a spiritual director—to help us pay attention to and respond to God's presence in our lives.

Even though I looked forward to meeting with Linda that first day, I was terribly nervous when I went to her home and to the room in her home that would be the sacred space for so many discoveries in my life. It was a bright, sunny room, overlooking the flower garden which her husband tended lovingly. The many window-sills were filled with rocks of all colors and shapes. Linda loved rocks and they were sacred for her, so she filled the space with them. The other walls were lined with books, many of them quite old, with that wonder-ful smell old books emit. Linda and I sat facing one another in large stuffed chairs, big enough for me to curl up in.

That first day we each shared a little about our hopes and wishes. I shared my own sense of brokenness and my wish to find the path that led to healing and whole-ness. Linda shared a little of her own philosophy and her way of working with directees. We were both test-ing the waters, seeing if we thought we would be able to work with each other. As we talked and found ourselves compatible, we agreed to meet monthly, for about two hours each time.

Over the next few years, as I worked with Linda, our time developed into a pattern. I would come, usu-ally full to the gills, with concerns, worries, discoveries, joys. We talked about God, about relationships, about my difficulty in finding a church community I liked, about work, about my past and present. Having found a place where I could openly discuss my understandings of God's place in my life, to ask Job's questions about why I suffered, to share my delight in finding God in various new corners of my life, I think I just talked and talked, and probably didn't give Linda much of a chance to say anything. After my talking slowed down, or as I began to repeat myself, Linda would begin to ask questions, the kind that helped me focus on the issues in new ways. Linda's ability to ask just the right question was uncanny. More often than not, one question from her would reframe my entire concern, showing it to me in whole new ways — ways full of opportunity and possibility. The question I hated the most, however, was: "Have you prayed about this?" I was not yet in the habit of any regular practice of prayer and inevitably, in the midst of some crisis or angst, would forget that praying (versus worry, anger, etc.) was another way of asking for God's help and response.

During the last half hour or so of our monthly time together, Linda would lead me in a guided meditation based on our discussion. I remember one very powerful day when I was feeling blocked by the demands of my world and the pain of my past, and felt unable to overcome the block. Linda asked me to let the blockage take some form in my imagination, and it took the form of an overwhelmingly large, darkly colored stone. (If you remember the monolith from the movie *2001*, that is close to what I imagined.) Over the course of the meditation, the monolith simply melted, and the healing of that block began. The meditations were not magic — they didn't heal everything then and there. But by using them over time, in my own prayer time as well as with Linda, many of them effected extraordinary levels of healing.

❧

What we each do and say with our spiritual directors, how often we see someone and for how long, varies according to the needs and interests of the people involved. Maybe the stories of various individuals will give you a sense of the variety of approaches.

"Our time together," writes Jonathan, "usually about ninety minutes, begins with my spiritual director ringing a chime three times, a period of silent centering prayer ending with a spoken prayer, followed by discussion in which my spiritual director usually asks probing and sometimes insightful questions. We conclude with a time of silent prayer and meditation ending with a spoken prayer. The space usually includes a small icon, burning incense, and a burning candle."

Eloise sees her spiritual director every other month for about two hours, over dinner. She writes a letter to her director in the months she does not see him and finds the letters an important aid to renewing and reviewing her own journey. When she and her director meet, the discussion often centers on the contents of the letters.

Beth lives in a rural area without easy access to a spiritual director, so she "meets" with her director monthly via the Internet. She posts a monthly letter to her director and receives a response. Though it seems an unusual arrangement to many, Beth points out that our Christian heritage is full of spiritual correspondence and direction, that this was considered normative at many times. The experience is a different one, however, as Beth points out. "In my previous two experiences [with spiritual directors] there would be a sense of both of us feeling together the breath of the Spirit in a particular direction. Online, this and similar things can't happen. Thus there can be a distance about it. I still think, though, that the parts of direction that have to do with things I've needed to be told over and over (like 'don't be so hard on yourself') are just as sacramental (in a broad sense) on the screen as in person." She also comments on the possible advantages and disadvantages of the lack of body language and tone of voice: "I can think of at least one time when that ambiguity has been an occasion of grace — I read one of his comments as having a tone like 'get a life,' which was exactly the kick in the pants I needed. Yet when I thanked him for that, he replied that he had meant to be comforting."

Other individuals find themselves happier with a

more structured director. Jackie has a director who assigns reading for her to do between sessions, usually a passage of Scripture. Their sessions take place in a retreat center where the director works and involve discussion around the passage and the impact it had, or didn't have, on Jackie.

Whatever the structure of the time together, most of spiritual direction consists of conversation. It is about sharing our questions, concerns, insights, and celebrations with someone who cares deeply about our spiritual life and growth. It is about letting ourselves be deeply known by someone else and finding ourselves in the process. As Margaret Guenther, an Episcopal priest and spiritual director, writes: "Only by letting ourselves be known to each other and to our deepest selves can we have the assurance that we are known by God."[3]

Finding a regular spiritual discipline has been one of the harder things for me to develop. Just as I have problems keeping my New Year's resolutions about exercise, I find myself "forgetting" to set aside regular times for my spiritual life. I go in spurts, finding times of great connection to, and conversation with, God, and times of total absence of both. That's not innately a bad thing — we all have times where our

---

3. Guenther, *Holy Listening* (Boston: Cowley Publications, 1992), 46.

spiritual lives are more in focus than other times. Unfortunately, though, because I did not have a regular practice for many years, the stress of my life often caught up to me when I wasn't looking, and it took much longer to find that quiet inner core again once I was so stressed out.

One of the advantages of seeing a spiritual director, for me, has been the accountability it provides. If nothing else, about a week before I saw Linda each month, I would begin to worry that I hadn't focused much on any of the issues we'd discussed, and I would make some space in my life for them. Linda most often suggested particular guided meditations to me, for my use in between our meetings. Many of them required consistent use to be helpful. For instance, my work life is sometimes quite hectic and stressful. Linda would help me through a guided meditation that had me sitting quietly by a beautiful lake, an image of great peacefulness for me. Then she might suggest that I take that image, in my imagination, into the middle of my work space — to imagine myself sitting quietly by that lake, but in the middle of the store. The first time I would try to do something like that, the lake would disappear as soon as I imagined that tranquillity in the middle of the store. Practicing it repeatedly, however, I could finally bring that peacefulness I associate with God's presence into my work space and reduce the stress I felt being there during busy times. Without the practice the problems persisted, so I was glad to have someone who would ask me about my progress on a regular basis. Linda never scolded; she never criticized me for not practicing. In fact, Linda always encouraged me to follow my own best instincts about developing a spiritual practice, and what that might mean for me. Nonetheless, it was good to have someone whose monthly presence brought me back to the importance of regular spiritual practice.

❧

Perhaps one of the greatest benefits of seeing a spiritual director is the help we get in finding, and keeping, a regular practice of prayer (or a discipline, as it is sometimes called). In the same way that recovering alcoholics gain support and encouragement from their AA sponsor, our spiritual director can be the guide to helping us find our own best way to talk with God, to build the relationship we have with God. There are dozens of different techniques that might be suggested by a spiritual director, more than can be covered here, but some of the most common ones follow.

Journaling: Journaling, as a technique, is popular in the culture as a whole right now, and no less so in spiritual direction. By keeping a written record of your thoughts and feelings, joys and frustrations, you can often begin to discern patterns in, and new understandings of, your life experiences. The journal becomes a record of your personal relationship with God. In much the same way that you might reread old letters to and from friends, you can reread your journal to understand how your relationship with God has grown.

Contemplation/meditational prayer: For many people meditation is a good way of quieting themselves so that they are able to listen to God. There are many different meditation practices, but finding one that matches your own abilities and inclinations, and practicing it regularly, can provide you with a place of deep quiet. Many find that even a short period of meditation on a regular basis, even meditation which is not entirely satisfactory at the time, aids the development of peacefulness that can be carried over into daily life.

Exercise: Others find that various physical activities are the best inroads to God. Yoga, an Eastern practice that consciously incorporates spiritual elements, works well for many people. Thich Nhat Hahn, the great Buddhist teacher, has also popularized the idea of walking meditation, or the practice of walking mindfully — with full attention to the present moment.

Spiritual reading: Reading various books or passages of Scripture, while dialoguing with the texts, is helpful to many. A particular technique, called *lectio divina,* which is a combination of meditation, slow and careful reading, and journaling, enjoys great popularity these days. (See chapter 6, on spiritual reading, for a fuller description of this practice.) A director can be particularly helpful in assisting you to select texts that might be suitable.

Retreats: Particularly for those of us with busy schedules, periodic retreats can be enormously helpful. Depending on your own personality and needs, a group retreat or a private and perhaps even silent retreat might be suggested. (See more about retreats in chapter 3 later in the book.)

The combination of these things, and other spiritual practices (such as community service, financial giving), can be combined and eventually become a set of resolutions (or Rule, in Christian terms). Rules, or set ways of living, were established originally for monks and nuns many centuries ago. A rule for your own life is more likely to be something you establish over a period of time and would likely include prayer practices, self-care, and your own goals for giving time and/or money to others who need help. My own rule, for instance, includes five twenty-minute periods of prayer and five twenty-minute periods of exercise each week, two church services of any sort each month, along with the percentage of my income I will give to charities and reminders about taking my vitamins and trying to maintain an attitude of kindness and service to all I meet.

The dreaded day was coming, and I knew it, but I sure didn't want to think about it. Linda's work — her writing and retreat work — was taking her all around the country and away from seminary teaching. It became increasingly hard for us to find times to get together, and we started seeing each other every other month at the most. At various times, she traveled overseas extensively, and we would take a hiatus for many months, writing an occasional letter during that time. But the day finally came when Linda had to stop seeing clients and give more of her time to retreat work and her books. It was not one of my favorite days.

Finding a new director was a very scary proposition to me. I'd found Linda quite by accident, or what seemed like an accident. She'd been incredibly important in helping me find healing pathways in my life. I'd come to rely on her. Setting out to find a new director, and starting all over with someone new, filled me with a certain amount of dread, and I put it off for many months, until a particular crisis in my life prompted me to get moving again.

As I started to talk with people who might be able to recommend a new director to me I was repeatedly asked: "What kind of person are you seeking?" For a variety of reasons, my associations with female therapists and spiritual directors had been more satisfactory than my work with male ones, so I was convinced I wanted to work with another woman. Since I hate driving with a passion, I wanted someone who was close by geographically. I wanted someone who was going to be available on a monthly basis to me, and someone who wasn't going to break the bank for me financially. And truth be told, I wanted someone just like Linda.

I spent a lot of time asking friends about directors they knew. I'd also asked one of our local priests for recommendations. Linda had suggested a person or two, but they both had too many clients to take on a new one at that time. I finally called a friend of mine, someone who heads up a professional society of spiritual directors, and asked him for recommendations. At the very end of his list was someone I knew only a little, a customer at the store and newly appointed to the faculty at one of our seminaries — and a man. If I've learned nothing else over the years, it is that God has a sense of humor. I had been so sure that I wanted to work with a woman as I searched out names and had resisted following up on any of the recommendations of male spiritual directors. I have no idea why, but when I heard Michael's name on the list of recommendations, I instantly knew that he would be the right person to work with.

Michael and I met a few weeks later to see if we thought the relationship would be a good one, and quickly decided that it would. Michael has been different from Linda, and though I would never have volunteered to give up seeing Linda, I am grateful for

Michael's guidance now too. There is a popular saying in spiritual circles: When the student is ready, the
teacher will come. Perhaps that applies to my work with
Michael, or perhaps it is because Michael asks different
questions than Linda asked, or perhaps I needed to do
the groundwork I did with Linda before being ready to
work with Michael. But Michael has been my guide and
companion for journeys into both darkness and light
and has guided me to vistas that I'd never glimpsed before. With Michael's gentle but firm guidance, I have
found places of forgiveness — of myself and others —
and a connection to God and the universe that seemed
impossible a few years ago.

We often find our spiritual directors, our teachers, are
not who we thought they were going to be. A friend
of mine, a minister who came from a very conservative
background, found herself questioning her theology and
feeling unappreciated as a woman clergyperson. The
director she sought out, to help her through these dilem-
mas, was a Catholic priest. Since Catholics don't ordain
women, it seemed like an odd choice, but she found him
very affirming of her ministry. He was the perfect choice
for her.

Perhaps you've heard the old phrase: God works in
mysterious ways. That's very true for the process of
finding that guide who can give you hints about find-

ing the path to God. Nonetheless, we can still do some thinking about what matters to us in a director before seeking one out.

An important question for many of us is the question of gender. Whole books have been written about spiritual direction for women, and there are legitimate reasons why any of us might choose a male or a female director. The patriarchal language of the church, and its historically male orientation, has been a source of deep wounding for many women — not to mention the men who have been forced to live according to unhealthy stereotypes. While there are many male spiritual directors with great sensitivity to those issues, some women will feel more comfortable negotiating that pain with a woman. Margaret Guenther, in her book for directors, *Holy Listening,* suggests that people who have been abused as children may find themselves more comfortable with a female director as well.[4] For others, finding a director of the same gender matters most. One woman I spoke to wanted to explore her issues around being single and felt she could do that better with another woman. Perhaps the most important thing is to listen carefully to your own inner voices on this issue, while maintaining an openness to other possibilities.

Something else to consider may be whether you want someone from a particular faith tradition, and whether

---

4. Guenther, *Holy Listening,* 136–37.

you would like that person to be clergy or not. Those who have been deeply wounded by the experience of church may feel more comfortable with a spiritual director who is not a member of the clergy. Other people report that having their director be a clergyperson matters immensely to them. One priest I have spoken to has a spiritual director who is from an Eastern tradition. This is another place to search our hearts, but remain open.

Finding a director is not always easy, but it need not be overwhelming. Checking with the minister or priest of a local church can be helpful. Roman Catholics and Episcopalians, in particular, have a strong history and appreciation of spiritual direction and can be good resources. If your town has a local seminary, or a retreat center of any sort, those may both be good sources for suggestions. There are also several professional societies throughout the country that may be able to make a recommendation. See p. 159 below for the names and numbers of these organizations.

The most important thing, in the long run, is finding someone with whom you feel comfortable talking. My own experience has been that the conversations I've had with my spiritual directors have been some of the best and hardest conversations I've ever had. In the beginning, even with my strong desire to talk about my spiritual life, it was hard to find the words, and talking about God felt awkward. Particularly if you are from a liberal church tradition, or grew up without a church background, talking about God feels almost akin to being declared insane. As I spent more time exploring my relationship with God, I began to understand my world differently. I began to have experiences, even mystical experiences, that were totally new and somewhat frightening. Talking about all of this, talking with my directors about what was deepest and, sometimes, darkest in my soul has never been easy. But they are some of the most honest conversations I've had. There have been some where I've felt more understood than ever before, and some where I've felt more vulnerable than I ever care to feel. Often the ones where I've been the most vulnerable have led to moments of clarity and understanding that astonish me, but none of that would have been possible without the gentle, careful, and caring guidance of directors I trusted.

One night, about fifteen years ago, I had a horrible dream. I dreamed that I had fallen into an endless dark tunnel, and that I was going to spend eternity falling into limitless darkness. It was a bleak time in my life, a time when I was just beginning to confront the woundedness of my family's history and its effect on me. For many months I dreamed that dream, and it exhausted me.

As fate would have it, this was also a time of spiritual awakening for me. I was discovering the power of prayer and beginning to be conscious of God's presence in my life. As I continued to dream that awful dream, one night a dim light appeared. As time went on, that light grew stronger and brighter. The image remains with me even now, all these years later, and is one I've shared with my spiritual directors.

In many ways it has been my work with spiritual direction that helps that light to grow ever brighter. God gave me the light originally, but my spiritual directors have helped me to stay focused on it. Tom taught me that spiritual directors cannot provide me with instant answers to all my spiritual questions. Linda taught me to quiet myself and open myself to God's healing images and words. Michael has taught me to believe in God's love for me. All have helped me focus on God, to let God's light grow brighter and bolder in my life.

− T H R E E −

Retreats

Every May I have the good fortune to take forty boxes of books to sell at a conference that meets at the Asilomar Conference Center, along the Monterey coastline in California. This year when I went a ranger was talking to a group of children about the sand dunes that sit between the beach and the conference center, and as I listened to the park ranger, I realized that retreats are a lot like those sand dunes.

According to the park ranger, the dunes were originally created by wind blowing sand from the beach. Over time, however, as the wind continued, it threatened to destroy the very sand dunes it had created. In order to protect the dunes, rangers roped off the area and built boardwalks so that people could stroll through the dunes without damaging the fragile wildflowers and plants that grew there. They also added an irrigation system, to give the new plants sustenance. Seven years ago, when I started visiting Asilomar, the dunes didn't have much life on them. Looking at them this year, after two winters where we've had a good deal of rain, there are lots of plants and wildflowers and even some small pine trees growing there. The roots from the plants hold the sand and soil in place and keep the wind from blowing the dunes away. And the deer and other wild animals now feed on the plants, relying upon the dunes as a place for food.

Retreats function in much the same way. We "rope off" some space and time, focus ourselves on God, and, often, we experience important growth. Like the fragile root systems of the dune plants which go deeper into the ground, finding water and nutrients to support fuller life, we, too, can find new perspectives, new understandings, and a deeper home in God which makes it possible to live a richer life. The increased richness in our own lives inevitably adds richness to the lives of those around us. Like the dune plants, too, this connectedness to God requires constant tending. Retreats alone, without any attention to our spiritual life outside of the retreat, will not result in a long-term romance with God. The dune plants could not be roped off for a week, or even a year, and still bloom as they do today. But retreats, as one piece of our spiritual lives, can be powerful and important times of growth and encouragement.

While sometimes we go on retreat on a regular schedule, and for no particular reason, mostly we go out of a need to stop, rest, and renew or develop our relationship with God, or perhaps to seek God's help with discernment over an important decision. The busier and perhaps the more "successful" we are in the world's eyes, the more we may need times of retreat.

These periods away need not be long — a weekend or a few days will do when a longer retreat isn't possible or desirable. What matters is that we get away for brief periods of rest, renewal, and reconnection. Retreats reset us. They help us see our lives from new perspectives, and they prepare us to live in our everyday world more fully, from a more centered place, a place that is closer to God.

Retreats can be times of solitude with God, or periods of exploring one's relationship with God within a community setting. Both are powerful tools in helping us stay focused on the things that matter most in our lives. They allow our overactive minds to quiet down for a while, to listen for a change. New surroundings, silence, and a time away from our busy lives allow us some time for our romance with God.

Solitary Retreats

"What is it going to be like? What will I do to fill my days? What should I bring?" I am a world-class worrier sometimes, and I was full of concerns and questions before taking my first silent and solitary retreat. "You'll sleep a lot the first couple of days," everyone told me. Frankly, I was hoping for answers that would allay my fears a little more.

Though I was very nervous about a five-day silent retreat, I'd scheduled it because my mind was full to the brim with work, various volunteer projects, and schedules to meet. I was having trouble sleeping, spending my nights working out the next day's schedule, and trying to solve tomorrow's problems as I slept. About four months prior to this, I'd had a scare about my physical health, and I'd decided that I needed to refocus my life. No one ever died, as they say, wishing that they'd worked harder. But still, I was spending every waking moment, and most sleeping moments, thinking about work, doing work, or worrying about not working hard enough. I needed to get away from work, to be someplace where work was not permitted. I wanted a few days without ringing telephones, without e-mail, without staff, customers, colleagues, or even friends asking me for anything. I'd tried some vacations where I'd stayed at home and gotten some rest, but this time I didn't even want the possible distractions of cleaning the house, mowing the lawn, or playing games on my computer.

I also needed time to explore my relationship with God. During the time I'd been worried about the possibility of a tumor, I'd discovered a new closeness to God. I'd discovered that God was, indeed, very present with me, even — or especially — in times of fear and anguish. But the minute the scare was over and it was determined that I didn't have a tumor, I got right back to work. In fact, I needed to play catch-up on work that hadn't gotten done while I was off having tests and dealing with medical procedures. Even so, in the midst of the flurry of work and the Christmas season at the store, I was still aware of God's presence, and I wanted time to stop to explore that relationship more fully.

Friends told me a little of their silent retreats, and all spoke highly of the experience. It seemed like the perfect solution to my overcrowded mind — pure, unadulterated silence for a while. I'd heard of thirty-day silent retreats, but I was pretty sure that I wasn't up to thirty days of silence. I decided that even a whole week felt pretty intimidating, so I settled on five days.[1]

I wanted to be someplace with lots of space and natural beauty. I also wanted to be someplace where I had friends close by, so that I wouldn't have to go directly from a retreat center to the bustle, noise, and activity of an airport. In the midst of a particularly cold and rainy winter, I felt drawn to the desert — a good biblical sort of place to be drawn. Lots of things happen in deserts in the Bible. The desert is a place for journeys, often long and arduous journeys. It is a place for becoming something different, a place for facing and overcoming

---

1. Many people choose to go on retreat for a shorter period of time at first. Weekend retreats are not at all uncommon.

temptations. Because I had some friends in New Mexico, I settled on staying in a hermitage in a convent a few miles outside of Albuquerque.

I flew there on a Saturday afternoon and stayed with a friend for the weekend. He dropped me off at the retreat center first thing on a sunny and bright Monday morning in mid-March, and as he drove away, panic set in. Within seconds, I desperately wanted to get out of there, didn't know why I'd thought this was going to be a good idea in the first place. What in the world was I going to do for five whole days with no meetings, no phone calls to return, no agenda, no distractions?

That feeling of being uneasy with the quiet isn't unusual at the beginning of an extended time of silence. The transition between the bustle of daily activity and the instant cessation of it always jars. "Be still, and know that I am God!" the psalmist writes in Psalm 46, but that is much easier to say than to practice.

The convent was located on a few miles of desert, with mountains on the horizon in several directions. A hermitage is a small dwelling that allows for a moderate level of isolation. Mine was one of four, lined up in a row, each with an adobe wall around a small yard in front, giving us "hermits" a private place to sit outside if we wished. The hermitage itself was a small room, with a bed, an armchair, a desk, a small kitchenette, and a bathroom. One side of it was filled with a picture window, which overlooked the desert. My particular hermitage was the one dedicated to St. Teresa of Avila, so there was a picture of the saint on the wall and a brief biography of her. There was a prayer of welcome on my bed, and a list of instructions about operating the heat and air conditioning and about how to clean the hermitage before checking out at the end of my stay.

A nun showed me to my hermitage and gave me a few brief instructions about the one daily meal that would be served in the retreat house — some days lunch, and some days dinner. She told me about community worship times, if I cared to join in. She also promised to stop by once a day and bring simple foods so that I could prepare meals for myself as I wished.

The land around the hermitage was mostly open and empty space, with lots of places to walk. The convent was a little above Albuquerque, and at night the lights of the city twinkled in the distance below. During the day, the Sandia mountains which surround Albuquerque were visible. As the sun moved during the daylight hours, the color of the mountains changed, becoming a glowing pink at sunset.

Also on the property was the convent itself, a retreat center where the nuns and others conducted occasional group retreats, dorms for those attending retreats, and a small desert chapel that was open at all hours. A small, circular building, the chapel was simple and elegant, filled not only with the objects often found in Catholic churches — crosses, Bible, candles, and other religious items — but with wood and objects from the surrounding desert. During the day the patio around the chapel was a wonderfully sunny spot for quiet meditation. At night, the chapel was quiet and dark, lit only by candlelight, and I would often wander down the path from my hermitage to go sit quietly and pray there.

In the first few hours at the convent, I restlessly wandered around exploring the terrain, the chapel, and settling in to my surroundings. At the end of my tour, my watch read noon, so I made myself some lunch. I even washed the dishes after eating, though it isn't unusual for me to leave my dishes sitting on the counter for a couple of days at home. After that, I was back to wondering what I was going to do for the next four and a half days.

I am so accustomed to full and busy days, governed by the needs of the store, staff, and customers, that I had a hard time simply "being" instead of "doing." I walked around the desert a little, and then decided to take a nap, something I rarely do in my normal life. Even when I am exhausted and try to take a nap, I'm rarely able to sleep, and usually give up after a half hour of lying in bed pretending to sleep. So I was surprised when I woke up from my nap several hours later. My friends had been right: I slept almost twelve hours each of the first two days of my retreat.

I struggled through the first day, dealing with alternating senses of panic and restlessness, with the quiet and lack of schedule. I felt disoriented and confused without my schedule of appointments and my "to-do" list. Somehow or another I made it through the first day, going to sleep quite early — what else was there to do? — and waking with the sun the next morning.

In some ways, the early days of being on retreat are about tolerating boredom. Some of us practice formal meditation or prayer practices if we have them, or just sit in our surroundings watching the world unfold around us. In the early stages of a retreat, before our bodies and minds have slowed down a little, it can be excruciating to watch the hours creep by slowly. Enduring the boredom and frustration of the early days of retreat is as much meditation as is contemplation which leads to a sense of deep connection to God. Usually I slip back and forth between the two during retreat time, feeling the initial sense of boredom, finding connection to God, and flipping back into restlessness and boredom at times. Staying with the meditative practice, being quiet and avoiding distractions, however, is the only way I've ever found to truly quiet my thoughts for any period of time and allow myself to hear God's voice instead of the endless chatter in my head.

Slowing down and giving up the idea of a schedule and a to-do list is certainly one of the hardest parts of a silent retreat. By going on retreat where you have not brought lots of books, papers, work, friends, and family to distract you, you are making time to be mindful of your relationship with God. You are promising to do your best to avoid distractions, in favor of simply being with God and listening for what might develop. For that reason, we take very little with us on retreat. There is no reason to take fancy clothes. No one will see them. Bring what is practical and comfortable for the climate you expect. Take some leisure reading if you wish, or some reading that speaks to you spiritually, but not so much that it fills the days and evenings. Most retreat centers, convents, and monasteries will also have libraries where you can find books of interest. If you enjoy writing, take along a journal or notebook in which to record your thoughts, prayers, or dreams. Christian retreat centers usually provide Bibles in your quarters, but bring one along if you want a particular Bible or translation at your disposal. Some people also bring along their favorite icon, rosary, prayer stone, or some other object that helps them focus their prayers. Other than that, go with as little to distract you as possible. The less we have to do, the more we can pay attention to God and to God's call to us.

Convents, monasteries, and retreat centers are often wonderful places for these periods of silence in our lives. (See p. 160 below for a list of books describing various places you might stay.) Many of them provide hermitages set apart from the main buildings, and others will provide guest rooms or quarters within the retreat center itself. Hermitages often include a basic kitchen, with a hot plate or stove, a refrigerator, and a sink for preparing simple meals. Frequently, one meal a day will be served to retreatants. If several are eating that meal at the same time, or if the meal is eaten with the community, it is not unusual for the meal to be taken in silence, or for a member of the community to read from the Bible or a spiritual autobiography during the meal. Though it can feel awkward at first to be sitting in silence at a meal with others, you may soon come to appreciate the lack of distraction and the lack of need to come up with small talk.

Over the next few days, I relaxed and began to enjoy the lack of structure in my days. I decided to read the book of Isaiah in the Bible left in my hermitage. Isaiah is one of the more dramatic books of the Bible. Written before, during, and after the Babylonian exile, Isaiah is full of prophetic visions, of harangues against oppressors and those who do not follow God's ways, and of dreams and promises of what it will be like to return home and be in God's good graces once again. I'd read parts of Isaiah for a class once, but never the whole book, and I'd meant to do that for some time. In the earlier parts of the book, Isaiah berates the people of Israel for their lack of faithfulness. As luck would have it, there was a desert storm in Albuquerque that day. Reading Isaiah's lengthy condemnation of the people in the midst of strong desert winds that blew gigantic tumbleweeds about as if they were lint was a dramatic experience I'm unlikely to forget.

My days were filled with lots of walking as well. With the exception of the one day it stormed, the rest of the days were cool, but sunny and beautiful. So I spent a lot of time walking in the desert, fearful at first of all the desert animals and insects I was afraid I would meet, but never encountered. One of my favorite walks was out a long dirt road that stopped at the fence on the boundary of the property. From that particular spot, the view of the mountains was clear and unobstructed, and I would sit in the dirt there for hours and just watch and pray. The Sandia mountains often focused my prayertime. They rise quite high above the city of Albuquerque, with an exquisite profile, solid and steady. They became a symbol of stability and majesty, and I watched them for hours wondering how I might be as solid and quiet as the mountains.

Sometimes, in the evenings, I read novels. I'd decided not to bring any books on spirituality or religion with me, since I read these books for a living and I knew they would feel too much like work. Fiction is one of my great pleasures in life, and I come away from that alternate world feeling rested and refreshed. I rarely have time to read for pure pleasure, given the large number of books I have to read professionally. Reading a couple of novels was one of the great delights of my time away.

Such was the outward structure of my five days at the retreat center. The interior landscape of that time is harder to describe but is what draws me back to times of silence in my life again and again. Sometime around the end of the second day, I was surprised and delighted to discover that the constant chatter in my mind was gone. Usually, when I try to meditate and clear my mind for short periods of time, I experience the frustration of endless thoughts and concerns galloping through my mind uninvited, and it is nearly impossible to turn them off. When I can be silent for a couple of days, however, the thoughts seem to disappear of their own free will, and I suddenly discover that my mind is quiet and receptive. Instead of issuing constant instructions, my mind finally rests quietly, waiting expectantly for my own deeper voices, and for God.

For many of us, this is the value of retreat time. Aside from all the wonderful benefits of resting and refreshing the body and mind, retreat time can allow you to establish or reestablish your connection to God and can be a space in which you are able to hear clearly and see your life and world in new ways.

On that particular retreat, I became exquisitely aware of how many gifts God has given me in this life. Gifts, not in the sense of material things, but of skills and talents. Of wonderful people in my world, friends and colleagues that I enjoy and respect, who make me laugh, and who care deeply about me. My awareness of these gifts in my life overwhelmed me suddenly, as did my own sense that I had not valued those gifts properly. I realized that I'd taken my gifts for granted. I'd assumed that everything I had was the result of what I'd earned, rather than seeing that God had gifted me greatly, and that gratitude, rather than arrogance, was the appropriate response.

For perhaps a day, I found myself in tears off and on through the day. Though I didn't feel any condemnation from God for my many years of arrogance, I felt deeply sorry, and the tears helped to express my sorrow to God. On the fourth day of the retreat, I began to make a list of ways in which I might refocus my life as a servant of God, rather than a person who believes she controls her entire existence. I wrote notes for myself on expressing gratitude toward God and others and about learning greater patience with all. I do not always see others as being gifted by God, and I asked God for the patience to help me see their gifts. I also wrote down some hopes for my own prayer life, including the goal of setting up a prayer corner in my house — a sacred space where I could go to pray, where nothing else was done. I did set up a prayer corner when I got home and put in it a stone I found in the Albuquerque desert that will always remind me of the peace I found there. I wish I could claim as much success in finding the gift in every person I meet, or in expressing my gratitude to God for my gifts. I've made some progress, but I still have lots to learn.

❧

My own retreat experience, that first time, was a very positive experience. I had been with a spiritual director for many years before I went on retreat and was ready for some time of undirected silence. The silence, however, can be intimidating and can sometimes lead to overwhelming or painful experiences. In particular, unresolved emotional issues may surface, and the solitude may magnify their impact. Within retreat centers, monasteries, or convents, there are many resources that support those on retreat, and these are usually available to retreatants free or for minimal charge or donation. The retreat community itself may be an indirect resource to you. Particularly in monasteries or convents, there is a community of people of some size that surrounds you, and it is likely that they are holding you in prayer while you are with them. In various convents and monasteries, and sometimes even in retreat centers, there are daily worship services celebrated by the community, and retreatants are usually welcome to attend.

Finally, there is usually someone designated as the retreat master or spiritual director of a retreat center, and this person can be a powerful guide for you. Many retreat places also offer spiritual direction to those on silent retreat. You can see a director once a day, once during your stay, or not at all, but many find the help and guidance of a director invaluable to their retreat experience. Even if you see a spiritual director regularly, the change in perspective that comes with a temporary director can be enormously helpful. The spiritual director can be a lifeline if you find yourself having disturbing dreams or feeling troubled or uncomfortable for any reason. A rule of thumb might be that it is probably best to plan to see a director if you have never done a silent retreat before. If you find the experience unnecessary or unhelpful, you do not need to continue.

Once you have found quiet places on your retreat, leaving them can be a jarring experience. Plan for some transitional time at the end of your retreat. In Albuquerque a friend picked me up at the end of my retreat, and we spent a day driving from Albuquerque to Ghost Ranch, a stunningly beautiful conference center in New Mexico that is the location for many of Georgia O'Keeffe's paintings. We spent the day talking, driving, seeing a tourist spot or two, and walking in the canyons at Ghost Ranch. The slowly paced day, with little on the agenda but quiet conversation, was a good way to move out of my retreat space and back into the more social world. Planning something of that nature can help cement your retreat experience and allow you some time to move back into the mainstream more easily.

That first silent retreat was a major turning point in my life. I'd had trouble sleeping all of my life — always lying awake for an hour or more before falling asleep at night and feeling frustrated about not sleeping. During the retreat, I started sleeping deeply and long, and that has continued to be the case since that time. I discovered there a quietness in my soul that I had never known was possible, and in that silent space I was able to see God's great gifts in my life and found a heartfelt sense of gratitude for them. There were no great booming voices from the heavens, no burning bushes, but I heard some of God's call to me all the same in that desert in Albuquerque.

Community Retreats

While the seclusion of a solitary retreat is perfect at times, there are other times when you want either less isolation or perhaps a slightly more structured or focused retreat. Maybe you are interested in learning more about a particular type of prayer, a particular saint's theology, or some other aspect of Christian life. Churches, retreat centers, convents, and monasteries offer a variety of programs for groups who want to examine a subject or just be in silence together, overnight, over the weekend, or for longer periods. For those who are new to Christian spirituality, these can be wonderful places for learning about faith and spiritual life.

I remember one group retreat where this was so for me. First of all, I have to say that I much prefer solitary time away from the world to group retreats. My work puts me in touch with people constantly. Though I enjoy the people and would not be without them, I look forward to times away when I can relax in solitude and quiet. But a friend of mine kept inviting me, each year, to a women's retreat held annually at the end of February. February is one of the times of the year that I generally feel most stressed. By February each year, I've had an unrelenting workload for several months, and I can be downright antisocial by the end of the period. And perhaps it was *because* I was so tired and stressed and ready to stop working, that I decided to go with her one year.

Though the retreat didn't begin until five o'clock on a Friday afternoon, we left early enough to get to the retreat center — a Catholic center about an hour away from home — in time to settle in and relax a little before everyone gathered. For me, that was a nice way of providing some break between the busy morning I'd had at work and the slower, more quiet time I expected to have on the retreat. Just as is true with silent and solitary retreat time, having some time to shift gears and move from one world to another is essential.

About five that afternoon, we all met together for the first time. Susan, my friend, knew almost everyone in the room, since she'd been attending the retreat for several years. For many of them, it was an annual reunion, and they looked forward to the time together. For my own part, I felt awkward. I knew Susan, and the retreat leader was also a friend of mine, but I knew no one else, and I turn reasonably shy in situations like these. Luckily, we'd all been asked to bring some hors d'oeuvres to share, and getting a plate of food and a glass of wine to drink gave me something to do for at least a few minutes. I spent a large part of the next hour hanging near the two people I knew, letting myself be introduced to others, and trying not to feel too awkward in a room full of folks who mostly knew each other and were catching up on each other's stories.

After dinner, the group gathered for our first formal session, led by Jenny, an Episcopal priest. Jenny introduced the subject of our retreat more fully. We would spend the weekend looking at images of women in the Gospels, exploring what they said to us about women's relationships with Jesus and, by extension, what they might reveal about our own relationship with Jesus. In advance of the retreat, Jenny had called and asked me to draw on my professional expertise and bring along a selection of books about women in the Gospels, and also some books by scholars of the Jesus Seminar[2] that dealt with images of Jesus. Memories of show-and-tell in grade school came to mind as I spent a little time telling the group about the books and making them available to those who wanted to look at them during the weekend. At the end of the session, Jenny gave us a list of passages where women's stories in the Gospels were found so that we could begin reading about them if we wished. We were asked to go in silence then, and to keep silence until the following morning at breakfast.

Where some of the anxiety of solitary retreats comes from being without a schedule or a to-do list, some of the awkwardness on group retreats can come from being with a group of people you either don't know at all, or barely know. We are suddenly going to spend lots of time talking about our spiritual lives and our understandings with a group of strangers! Or, as in the case of a church retreat, these are folks we may know casually from church, but the group retreat presents the opportunity to know these people in a very differ-

---

2. The Jesus Seminar is a group of scholars who have analyzed the words and works of Jesus, as reported in the Gospels and other sources, with the goal of determining which of the words and deeds might be closest to the actual historical Jesus. Their work has been highly controversial in some circles. In others, it has opened up conversation and given many the opportunity to wrestle with their images of Jesus and how those apply to their faith lives.

ent and perhaps deeper way. It no longer matters that we are bookstore managers, accountants, cashiers. Our professional roles, and perhaps even our family roles, are of little or no use to us on retreat. We have the opportunity, and the challenge, of just being ourselves for a few days, naked before God. It is no wonder that many of us feel some anxiety about going on retreat, even when we know the benefits.

For most of us short retreats, rather than longer events, are the most convenient or obvious way to explore retreat time. Many of them begin on a Friday evening after work, and end around lunch time on Sunday. The first evening is often spent in ways that allow the participants to get to know one another a little and to explore the theme of the retreat. It is also a time for giving out information about weekend logistics and facilities. The informational part of the evening is most often followed by either some time for socializing or, as was true for my retreat, a period of group silence.

I spent some time that evening, in the silence of my room, looking up the New Testament passages where women encountered Jesus. Of all the passages, the Emmaus passage from Luke grabbed my attention. In the story, two people are walking down the road after the crucifixion of Jesus. Jesus encounters them on the road, and they walk with him for some time, unaware of who he is. They finally realize it is Jesus when he breaks bread with them over a shared meal. Though we mostly assume that the travelers were men, Jenny had pointed out that the narrative does not indicate if the two travelers on the road are men or women, that there is evidence to indicate that they might well have been female. I identified with the story; if I met Jesus face to face I would not be surprised if I didn't recognize him either.

I looked through some of the other stories that evening too, but mostly I was tired. I found that without the television to turn on, no housekeeping to do, no e-mail to answer, I was ready for bed at an early hour. I took advantage of one of the great benefits of retreat time: sleeping.

The morning found us all gathering for breakfast in the dining room. We'd been silent since the previous evening, but broke our silence over breakfast, and over coffee spent time learning more about each other. I remember one woman, in particular, had borrowed a commentary from me, one that looked at Bible stories from women's perspectives. She'd spent lots of time looking through it the night before and had never seen anything like it. She was fascinated at this new approach to the Bible and talked very animatedly about it with me. As a group, we were beginning to know one another a little better, and the conversation was going a little deeper.

After breakfast, our morning session together was spent exploring the passages that Jenny had given us the previous night. Without spending a lot of time on each, we read through each reference and talked briefly about each woman's contact with Jesus. In the midmorning, Jenny suggested we pick one of the passages and spend some time with it. Though we could do what we wished with it, she suggested it might be helpful to place ourselves in the story we chose and write a dialogue from the perspective of one of the characters. We had a few hours to do that, disbanding around 10:30 that morning and meeting again after lunch around 1:30.

The structure of our retreat was not an unusual one. After some introductory time the first evening, the days are often divided between group discussion and exploration time, and some time for either reflection or recreation. When a retreat explores a specific subject, exercises may be suggested for retreatants' use. A word of caution about instructions or suggestions given to you during a retreat: while the exercises or readings suggested by the retreat leader are usually very helpful or instructive, there are times when you feel guided in a different direction or when the exercises don't seem to work for you at that time. If you feel a strong pull toward a different exercise, reading, or activity, there may be a good reason for that feeling and for acting on it. Retreat leaders often give retreatants permission to follow their own inner voices. Whether the leader remembers to say this or not, it is generally acceptable to follow your own instincts about what will be good for you, unless it involves an activity that will be disruptive to the rest of the group.

Because the weather was sunny and warm and the retreat center surrounded by gardens, I took advantage of the time to walk around the grounds. Because being Catholic was not a part of my upbringing, I found myself looking curiously at the retreat center. The gardens were full of statues of Mary, various saints, and Jesus, all clearly intended to spur devotional thoughts. Many of them were placed in private alcoves or spots, with a bench nearby so one could sit and reflect. There was also a walk clearly marked with what is called the Stations of the Cross, markers which commemorate key parts of the story leading up to Jesus' crucifixion. I wandered around looking at all of these things, many of them unfamiliar to me, and let my mind wander a bit.

As I wandered, I thought about the stories of women we'd heard that morning and wondered which of them was most like my own relationship with Jesus. I'd been sure, the night before, that I would use the Emmaus story from Luke for my reflection, but it was no longer calling me strongly this morning. I found myself pulled more strongly to the stories of Mary and Martha that appear in Luke 10 and John 11.

In the first story, Mary and Martha, sisters, are hosting Jesus in their home. Mary is sitting at Jesus' feet listening to him teach, while Martha is busy trying to be hostess to all the guests who are also listening to Jesus. Martha finally complains to Jesus and asks him to rebuke Mary and get her to help serve food and host the guests. Jesus, instead, rebukes Martha, telling her that she is fretful and anxious about unimportant matters.

This story is one often heard in churches, one that is often held up for one reason or another. All my life, I have understood that story to mean that paying attention to what Jesus is teaching is paramount, that nothing else matters more than that. But that day, I began to experience that anger of Martha at being scolded.

In the second story, Mary and Martha send word to Jesus that their brother, Lazarus, is dying. Jesus waits several days before journeying to Bethany, where he finds Lazarus already dead. Martha meets Jesus on his way to their home, and says to him: "Lord, if you had been here, my brother would not have died" (John 11:21). Mary, on the other hand, waits for Jesus to call for her, then goes to him, and kneeling before him says: "Lord, if you had been here, my brother would not have died" (John 11:32).

Both of the women have said the same sentence,

but in light of the earlier story in Luke, I experienced Martha as someone who was forthright and went out, willing to declare her anger at her friend, Jesus, who had not come to save her brother. She spoke clearly and honestly out of anger. Mary, on the other hand, seemed to me to be meekly waiting for Jesus to call her. She kneels in front on him, almost as if begging forgiveness for the hard sentence she says. In the next sentence, John tells us that Jesus saw her weeping, and I imagined her holding all of her sorrow and her anger inside, letting it come out as fearful tears, instead of bravely speaking her anger.

As the stories swirled around in my head, I became more and more angry and wrote a lengthy diatribe that Martha might have delivered to Mary. In it Martha told Mary to stop acting so meek and helpless, to stand up for what was good, just, and right. It was a wonderfully cathartic dialogue to write, very much a conversation to myself in some ways. It arose from my own experiences of being female and our culture's preference for meek and passive women, my own discomfort with anger, and my concerns about attitudes toward women in the church.

After lunch, we all met again to share our reflections on the passages. Most of us had written a dialogue of some sort. As we went through each of the Gospel passages, those who had written about that story read their dialogue. Each one revealed something about the woman who had written it, about her joys and fears, and about her own relationship to Jesus. Some of the stories were filled with humor, some with sadness or anger, while others were filled with devotion and love. We ran the whole range of human responses that day. As I listened to the reflections of each woman, I experienced a sense of connection with each. Several of us had written about the Mary and Martha stories, and I began to see the Gospel stories differently through each woman's eyes. Each of us wrestled with different issues in our lives and our worlds, but we all wrestled. And in all of the various perspectives, I became aware of the great gift we were to one another. The gifts varied from person to person. Some of the women brought quiet strength, born of decades of struggle and faithfulness. Others brought eagerness and the delight of discovering feminist perspectives that were new to them, that offered healing or depth. Others brought their pain, some of it quite acute, to share with the group. And through it all came a deep sense of care and concern, a support for each woman who sought to deepen her relationship with God and her world.

We closed our short retreat time with a brief worship service and the celebration of the Eucharist together. Rather than having Jenny serve each person, as is customary, we served one another, passing the bread and wine to our neighbors, a ritualized representation of the gifts we'd given each other that day.

One of the most fascinating things about retreats can be the difference between the way people feel at the beginning and at the end of the retreat. In silent and solitary retreats, we generally approach with our heads full of concerns and schedules, and often leave quiet and centered. In a group retreat, the participants, even if strangers to one another at the beginning, often feel a close bond; they have experienced the presence of God in one another. Through our connections with ourselves and with others, we renew our connection to God, and we see the world differently, even if only for a short period of time. It is that glimpse of a world infused with God, however, that brings many of us back to moments of retreat, that gives us hope and courage in our daily lives.

– F O U R –

Spirituality Online

"I'm in shock," I wrote to friends of mine, who would later read my words on a computer screen in their own homes. "My doctor called me tonight and told me I have a build-up of fluid in my spine that could be caused by a brain tumor. It's possible that the fluid is not related to anything important, but what if it *is* a tumor? I can't even imagine what to do next. Pray for me."

The news was quite a shock to me, and all the worst possibilities flooded into my head. I was thirty-eight at the time and hadn't thought about dying much. I certainly didn't feel prepared to face endless tests and treatments. I had spent some time talking with my neighbors and with friends over the telephone, repeating the news out loud, trying to make the reality sink in, but feeling deeply in shock. Late at night, alone in my home, I wrote of my surprise, and my fear, to a small group of e-mail friends.

What is amazing, in circumstances like these, is that the world goes on as if nothing has happened. For me, the whole world had changed in a flash. For everyone else, the world was the same place they had known yesterday. I needed a place where I could talk about and process the things that were happening to me — the new feelings and fears, my doubts and questions. There were many good and close friends living in Berkeley who provided wonderful care and support for me, taking me for tests and just listening to my fears and concerns. But there was also an online community of dear friends who gathered round and let me explore God's place in this new experience.

Since online communications are new to so many people still, let me say a little about my own community and how it works. The majority of my experience has been with a network called Ecunet, which is a consortium of individual networks sponsored by many Christian denominations (Presbyterian, Lutheran, Episcopalian, etc.) and other groups related to the church. As the network officially sponsored by many denominations, it consists of primarily theologically liberal to moderate Christians who are clergy, lay people, staff of various denominations, and other interested parties. Everyone on Ecunet is there out of an interest in religion, which makes the group a little more homogeneous than is usually the case on the large commercial networks. At the time of this writing, there are about twelve thousand people on Ecunet, which makes it a small community by computer network standards. The size of the network, however, also means that we get to know each other more easily than is sometimes possible in larger environments.

Conversations of all sorts occur on Ecunet. The "conversations" are not live ones, however, as is true on some computer networks; they are the equivalent of e-mail notes in meeting form. If you've signed up to join the conversation, you will see the notes that each person writes whenever you choose to sign on to the system. The conversations, or meetings, as they are generally called on Ecunet, can be about issues facing the church today, such as the church's stance on sexuality, homosexuality, racism, sexism, etc. Other meetings explore alternate theologies for the church, trying to blend liberation theologies or earth-centered (Gaia) theologies with traditional church doctrines. Still others discuss current television shows and the way religion is reflected in the popular media. We even have some meetings just for fun, where we discuss sports, our cats or dogs, Star Trek, and so on.

On most computer networks participants must stay within the topics established by those who run the system. On Ecunet, however, anyone can open a conversation on any topic and invite everyone (making it a public meeting) or only selected persons (a private meeting) to participate. For me, this is one of the most powerful features of the system, and I have often used private meetings to process job offers, changes, or crises in my life.

As I began to absorb the medical news about a possible tumor, I began a small private meeting on Ecunet as a place to examine my first encounter with my own mortality. Over the next few weeks, I reflected on my experiences and my questions with a group of six or seven close friends online. That group included some people who had been friends of mine while they were studying at the seminaries where I work, as well as others with whom I'd worked while serving on Ecunet's board of directors, plus some others I'd known mostly from my time online, rather than through face-to-face contact. I wrote to them of my shock and surprise, of my fears about being ill and maybe dying. I wrote of my anxiety about the MRI I needed to have for diagnostic purposes. Though I'd never experienced claustrophobia before, I'd had a powerful experience of it during the twenty-minute MRI that found the build-up of fluid. (MRIs are x-rays of sorts, taken while the patient lies still in a long and narrow tube.) The second one was going to take ninety minutes, and I could hardly face it. Members of my assembled group responded with their prayers, encouragement, support, and often with practical suggestions about questions to ask and ways to proceed.

My online community would certainly not have been

sufficient to support me during those difficult weeks. The hugs of friends, the transportation and support provided, were invaluable and could not be replaced by the virtual community. But the group assembled electronically provided me with a different and powerful kind of support. I could write to them at any hour of the day or night, whenever I needed to write. I had their support and their answers to my questions in written form, resident on my computer screen, where I could read and reread what had been written to me. In times past, perhaps that kind of correspondence was done by mail. Today, more and more, it is done via e-mail, providing instant communication and information, and almost immediate responses that are not possible by mail. In a crisis, it is sometimes difficult to keep track of what is being said and done, and it was wonderful to have notes that I could read, reread, and absorb as I was able.

❧

Support from the Christian community is one aspect of life online, but a more obvious benefit of computer networking is the easy access to information about Christianity. In her recent book, *Re-Discovering the Sacred*, Phyllis Tickle points out that Americans these days are reading more books on spirituality than has been true for many years. Her analysis of why people turn to books on spirituality could easily be true of the trend to learning spirituality via computer networks. She writes:

> ...Human beings are slow to change their public and social ways. As a species, we are especially slow to express aloud religious beliefs or visibly to pursue patterns that are too divergent from those of our community. We go public as a rule only after we are assured of finding some replacement group within our new practices, or else — rarely — we are completely overwhelmed by some incontrovertible personal conviction. Books, although they are a modern comfort and only recently available inexpensively and readily, are private. Books don't tell, especially in matters of the spirit. What the soul sends the mind in search of can be explored without prejudice in a book, and almost as significant, what the mind finds can then be checked, and evaluated, and tested against another book, and another, and another, ad infinitum and all with an almost perfect impunity.[1]

Reread that paragraph and substitute the words "computer networks" for any book references and you will have an apt description of what many of us are finding online. On any given day on Ecunet I can learn about almost any aspect of Christian spirituality.

---

1. Phyllis Tickle, *Re-Discovering the Sacred: Spirituality in America* (New York: Crossroad, 1995), 17.

Celtic spirituality, Gaia (earth-based) spirituality, centering prayer, praying the daily office (set prayers for morning and evening) are just a few of the recently popular topics.

I can also search the increasingly popular World Wide Web for religion and Christian spirituality sites as well, finding a wide diversity of perspectives.[2] Many Christian denominations maintain "home pages" or sites on the Internet that point you to all sorts of information about that denomination. Commercial networks, like America Online, CompuServe, Prodigy, and others have large areas devoted to Christian resources and conversation. In addition to that, I can join lists (world-wide Internet conversations) that discuss various topics, like Anglican spirituality, research of the historical Jesus and its impact on faith, theological or doctrinal concepts, or whatever interests me.

For the seeker who knows little about Christian spirituality and life, computer networks provide a fascinating vehicle to learning and discovery. They can even help us do that long before we may want to voice religious questions out loud. In fact, the person who wants only to explore can do so quite anonymously, without having to make his or her presence known and with-

---

2. An excellent book for beginners seeking religious resources on the Internet is Mark Kellner's *God on the Internet* (Foster City, Calif.: IDG Books, 1996). Kellner's easily read and useful book covers a wide range of resources across all faiths.

out contributing to the conversation at all unless he or she wishes to do so. For instance, I often feel that I should know everything there is to know about religion in my guise as a religious bookstore manager, and I feel that way despite the fact that I know this is impossible. So I sometimes simply observe conversations online — "lurk," in computer terminology — just to learn something about subjects where I know less than I'd like.

The information-providing features of the online community are evident to most people. They are what two authors, Lee Sproull and Sara Kiesler, refer to as "first-level effects." That computers allow us to share lots of information, quickly and efficiently, is obvious to the casual observer. More important, however, are the "second-level effects," the less visible consequences of being networked (or in communication) with other computer users. Sproull and Kiesler define second-level or social effects as those that affect what people pay attention to, what people they communicate with, and changes in how people depend on one another.[3] Computers connect people who would not otherwise have any reason or opportunity to contact one another. They connect people across wide geographical and cultural boundaries. This creates new opportunities and new perspectives for everyone involved.

---

3. Lee Sproull, Sara Kiesler, *Connections: New Ways of Working in the Networked Organization* (Cambridge: MIT Press, 1991), 4–5.

Perhaps the most fascinating of the second-level effects being discovered by those exploring their spirituality via computer networks is the ability to try on new voices, to write or think about new ways of being, and to see what they feel like. Some people are finding that this can be a life-changing experience.

Mark is one of those people. A baby boomer born in 1951, he grew up in a family that didn't attend church. It wasn't until he met and married his wife that he began attending church. Here is how he tells the story of his own spiritual awakening, via the computer network, which happened two years ago:

[My wife and I] joined a local Protestant church, and became active in the life of the congregation. While I was indeed active in the governing bodies of the church and in various other congregational activities, my spiritual life wasn't progressing very fast or far. I had what I would now characterize as a "comfortable" faith.

Through my involvement with some committee work, I was introduced to Ecunet and the online faith community. I was new to computers, and new to modems. [Modems permit computers to "talk" to one another over telephone lines.] What I found in the Ecunet community, however, excited me. People were openly discussing matters of faith and theology! I began to learn more about the personal faith of the people in the online community. The amount of raw information available to me about Christianity and the reformed faith began to grow dramatically.

Throughout this time, I was slowly coming to a realization that my life had been filled with signs of God's grace. But I still wasn't sure of what God was calling me to do. Then, in 1994, through Ecunet, I experienced a breakthrough. Someone started a meeting titled *Call Stories*. The organizer of the meeting wanted people to write about how they heard God's call. I joined the meeting and started reading the notes as they came in. One night, after reading about an individual's call, I sat at the computer and reflected on what I surely knew was God's presence in my life. I felt the overwhelming urge to start writing about what I had experienced and what I was struggling with. That night, I wrote a note to the meeting that tried to explain what I had experienced over my life. And believe me, I had never written or even spoken about these experiences to anyone before. And yet I knew that I was putting this note out in cyberspace with my name attached to it, for potentially thousands to see. I knew I had entered a new phase of my life.

The impact of this meeting on me was dramatic. I started to open my life more fully to God and ex-

plore what He was calling me to do. To be honest,
I'm still not certain what the answer is. But I'm a
heck of a lot closer! I have a different, closer relationship to God and Christ than I had before. I've
continued to learn more about my faith through
the network. I continue to experience new ideas
and new possibilities through this medium. Could I
have done it without the use of a computer? Honestly, I don't know. The support I received and
continue to receive through the caring, committed
Christians on this system adds tremendously to my
life.[4]

Years later, Mark still tells this story as if it were the
central story of his life. Clearly, it holds great power
for him.

Others share experiences similar to his. Andy, who
has struggled through a difficult life, with occasional
contact with the church, found his way back into
church life through his recovery from alcoholism via Alcoholics Anonymous. His early experiences with church
as a child were sporadic, with periods of intense church
activity, followed by periods of no family involvement
in church at all. The major influence on him was the
Episcopal Church, which is the church he came back to
as an adult. Through Ecunet, however, he is learning
new styles of praying and new depths of prayer:

---

4. Personal correspondence, February 13, 1996.

In the church where I grew up our prayers were "ready made" in the Book of Common Prayer. We read, said, mumbled, jumbled, and bumbled our way through the same prayers every Sunday. The words were immutable, unchanging, and timeless (well, until they revised the Book of Common Prayer!). Those prayers still reverberate in my memory. In times of stress, the words come to mind unbidden. The Episcopal Church does not have a tradition of do-it-yourself prayer. I barely knew there was such a thing. As a result of Ecunet and the examples I see set by members of other denominations, I now pray extemporaneously more than by rote. At many notes I read in meetings, I pause and offer a quick prayer for the persons or situations mentioned. In some cases I feel moved to write a brief prayer....I am astonished at the power of such prayers not only apparent in so many felicitous outcomes later described in the meetings, but also for relief of my own stress and apprehensions of the day. I find if I am praying for others, I am freed from focusing on my own petty problems. What a gift![5]

Free-form prayers, rather than the established ones commonly read from the Book of Common Prayer or the ones provided in AA resources, were new for Andy,

---

5. Personal Correspondence, February 18, 1996.

and not something he would have tried if he hadn't been online. The daily practice of that prayer, in response to requests posted online, not only aided those asking for prayer, but helped Andy heal as well.

Many computer networks have an area set aside for the kinds of prayer requests that helped Andy learn to pray his own prayers. For some, these kinds of forums are their first exposure to intercessory prayer — prayers on the part of others. People write (post) requests for prayer for themselves or others in their lives, or for distressing events in the world, and others post responses to those requests. The majority of people who participate in these kinds of forums, as is true of most conversations online, tend to simply read the notes and make whatever private response they wish to make, without sending notes back into the conversation. Others make a written response to every request for prayer that is posted, even if it is a short note that simply says, "I'm praying for you."

The experience of asking for prayer in a forum such as this can be powerful. Receiving notes from all over the country, or even various places around the globe, can leave you with a powerful sense of connection to others that is difficult to describe. It is not unusual for people in prayer meetings to report that they have felt the strong presence of the community after asking for prayer.

The experience of being in prayer for others around

the country, and even around the world, can also help to undo the parochial or geographical perspectives we sometimes hold. I remember being in a class on prayer once where the instructor asked us to imagine widening circles of people we might pray for. He began by asking us to pray for someone very close to us, then moved to close friends, and then asked us to extend the circle of prayer to include people in our local community, church, or job. For me, that meant a shrinking of the circle, since I include, among my close friends, many around the country with whom I correspond regularly.

Computer networks and their prayer forums have also become powerful places to process the sadness we feel when a tragedy happens somewhere in the world. The destruction of the Challenger space shuttle in 1986, for instance, generated a full service of mourning on Ecunet's predecessor, a system called Unison. Within a day of the explosion, Unison members were able to read and respond to a full service of prayers, Scripture, sermon, and even a "coffee hour" where everyone could talk about their feelings of sorrow. The bombing of the Federal Building in Oklahoma, earthquakes in various parts of the world, and other disasters are quickly reported online, and communities form to pray for victims or to work on sermons that address the pain people feel. Likewise "Prayer Chapel," one of the longest-running prayer forums on Ecunet, began as a result of the taking of U.S. hostages in Iran.

Like Andy and Mark, I have had some powerful moments of awakening as a result of my time on computer networks. Perhaps the most powerful one came as a result of the support of my online community while I was waiting to learn if I had the tumor or not. For years before that, I'd been a part of various prayer meetings on Ecunet. For the most part, I "lurked" (read notes but didn't respond) in those public prayer meetings. The sheer number of prayer requests sometimes overwhelmed me, not to mention the misery and suffering that was represented in the requests and reports. In large part, however, I lurked because I wasn't really sure that praying for others accomplished anything. In my midthirties I had had a car accident that toppled my understanding of faithfulness. Before the accident, I had convinced myself that if I was a good person, God would protect me, watch over me. And yet, I'd been in a serious car accident that totaled my car and resulted in some small plastic surgery for me. It was clear to me after that that God could not insure that bad things wouldn't happen to us. So why pray to God on behalf of ourselves or others?

With my small e-mail group assembled around me for the two weeks it took for medical tests to be done, I wrestled with this issue. I'd asked my e-mail group for their prayers, without any expectation that this would accomplish anything specific. Another online friend asked a small group of mutual friends for their prayers online. My next door neighbor, a dear friend, had also added me to our church's prayer chain, and I knew that a dozen or so people in our parish were praying for me there too. I didn't think that anyone's prayers would convince God to prevent me from having a tumor of some sort, or convince God to make the situation less serious. I'd asked for their prayers, and let others ask for prayers on my behalf, because that's what people are supposed to do in this situation, and I couldn't think of anything else to do anyway. I was too exhausted to pray for myself. I needed others to do it for me. They prayed, and I waited for the next MRI which would give us more answers.

For the first few days after the doctor's call, I walked through my days in a thick fog. Unable to know the future and unable to comprehend the variety of possibilities, I was emotionally numb most of the time. Alternately, I would begin shaking or crying out of deep fearfulness. I wasn't able to pray much in those first days. Physically I was too tired to pray, and spiritually I just had no idea what to say to God, so I wrote to those online of my fog and confusion. As the days went on and word spread online, notes came from friends and colleagues who had served with me on Ecunet's board of directors. From Baltimore, Chicago, New York, Indiana, Ontario, Geneva, London, and elsewhere they wrote. "We're praying for you, Debra," they said, "and for the doctors and those caring for you too."

As I was able, I wrote to my small group assembled online not only about the fog, but about the dreams I was having, about my fears, about my own inability to pray at that time. They listened well and sent notes of encouragement and support. They reminded me that they were praying for me and would continue to be there for me as needed. And gradually, as I read their notes over those two weeks, I began to experience a very physical sense of these people's prayers surrounding me. I began to feel wrapped in a blanket of their prayers and concern for me. Without being able to understand intercessory prayer in any intellectual sense, I started to experience its power emotionally and spiritually. As the days continued, I began to understand these feelings as God's presence with me, through the people who cared for me, via the computer and those in person both. I began to know that God was so powerfully with me that there was nothing that I could not manage with God's help. That if lots of tests and treatments were the next thing on my to-do list, I would be given the strength to bear them. That if I was going to die, I would be able to do that with much less fear than I'd previously thought possible. All of this felt a tad overdramatic at the time, and in the maelstrom of all the emotions that went with these few weeks, I found myself unwilling to talk about these feelings out loud. One night, however, I wrote them to my small e-mail group. I sent my thoughts out to everyone with great fear and trepidation, wondering if they would think that I'd gone over some emotional edge. The responses I got back told me that I wasn't losing my mind. Rather, I was finding new depths in my relationship with God, and my friends were honored to be witnesses to that process. With some new strength and confidence in my relationship to God, I could then turn to my friends locally and begin to speak aloud my new understandings and feelings.

Getting involved on a computer network may take some negotiating at first, particularly if this is entirely new for you. Ecunet as a network is almost entirely religious in nature, making it easy to find conversation about Christian or religious subjects. On commercial networks, such as America Online or Compu-Serve, there are areas dedicated to religious conversation. Many of the commercial networks offer trial memberships, or a certain amount of time online for free, which you can use to see if you can find a compatible community of seekers online.

Lest computer networking seem like the perfect and ultimate solution to finding Christian community and deepening your understanding of and relationship with

God, let me issue a few cautions. Because computers make it possible to get instant answers and feedback, there is a tendency to assume that you will always get what you need instantly. That assumption can turn into the tyranny of the computer for you and for your correspondents, when you always expect instant answers or feel you have to give instant responses. Communicating by computer also takes a little practice. There are conventions to learn, just like there are in other forms of communication. You are also experiencing people's words without body language or tone of voice, which sometimes leads to misunderstanding. Lastly, there is a tendency to forget that lots of people may be reading what you write. As you type away quietly in your own home, remember that lots and lots of people may be reading your notes, including people who know you, work with you, or are friends of friends. Don't type things online that you wouldn't want these people to know if you are not sure who is reading.

With all of these cautions in mind, however, computer networks and communities can become safe places to try on new ways of understanding ourselves and our relationships to God and one another. Very little research has been done on this topic so far, though the prevalence of computer networks will spur more work over the next few years. But the third section of Sherry Turkle's book *Life on the Screen: Identity*

in the Age of the Internet, touches on this subject.[6]
A sociologist and clinical psychologist working at the
Massachusetts Institute of Technology, Turkle explores
how people use MUDs — computer games where they
create their own personas online — to explore aspects
of their own identity. Online conversations of the sort
we've explored here are not the same as MUDs. We are
not creating complete personas and worlds in the same
way that Turkle's subjects do. But like those who play
in MUDs, many of us do explore aspects of our personalities and try on new understandings online. Mark was
able to discern aspects of God's call to him after reading
about other people's experience of being called. Andy
learned how to form his own prayers and found a way
to care more deeply for others, while moving his focus
away from his own problems. I discovered the power of
praying for others in my own experiences online. This
is a powerful feature of online life and it is becoming
more common to use computer communities as a sort of
transitional space.[7] For those of us exploring Christian
spirituality, whether for the first time or as we deepen
our spiritual understandings, we can use the computer
as a place to try on new words and new understandings

6. Sherry Turkle, *Life on the Screen: Identity in the Age of the Internet*
(New York: Simon & Schuster, 1995). Part 3 of this book, "On the Internet," has an excellent discussion of what kind of personalities individuals
create on MUDs and how they integrate or fail to integrate aspects of their
MUD personalities into their real lives.

7. Turkle, *Life on the Screen,* 262.

within the confines of a supportive Christian community. Once we feel that we have found what we need, we can begin to take these new realities into our daily lives beyond the computer screen.

– F I V E –

Prayer Groups

Andrea, a friend of mine, called me up one day. "I feel like my prayer life could use some help and support, and I'm thinking of forming a small women's prayer group. What do you think?" I thought it was a great idea. It was early December when she called, a time when we were both being bombarded by holiday activities and heavy work loads. My own prayer life was getting shunted off into the corner with the press of work, and I, too, needed a place that might serve as a regular reminder of the importance of prayer in my life, a place where I might experience support and encouragement in my spiritual life, and offer it to others. Over the next month, Andrea contacted some other women who we thought would be interested, and seven of us met for the first time in the middle of February.

At our first meeting, we each shared a little about how we felt about our own spiritual lives, and what our hopes were for a prayer group. I was just beginning to write this book at that time, and I talked about my fears about that, and asked everyone to hold me in prayer while I worked. Many of us expressed our distress that our prayer lives were often on the bottom of our lists of things to do instead of at the top. We talked, too, about how few places we had to talk about our spiritual lives, and how much we would value the time and space to talk about where we felt God was leading us in this life.

As a group, we are diverse in ages and interests. We range in age from somewhere around the midthirties to the midsixties. Some of us have full-time jobs, others work part-time, while others spend much of their time doing volunteer work. Some of us are single, others are raising families, and still others have grown children and even grandchildren. We have come out of a variety of mostly Protestant backgrounds, though our group includes one woman who is an Orthodox Christian.

The diversity of age, experience, and perspective adds richness to our experience. Where I might see something one way, someone else will bring in an entirely different perspective. One evening, for instance, one of our group was discussing forgiveness and how difficult she found that with particular people. None of us had anything to say that seemed to be particularly helpful until one woman quietly said: "Forgiveness is an act, not a state of mind." The statement brought a whole new perspective to the conversation, as we talked about whether or not we could forgive someone even while knowing that we were still angry at the person or hurt by their actions.

I particularly enjoy being in a group that includes women whose life experiences are vaster than mine, whose additional twenty years have taught them things I do not yet know. Watching some of the older women in the group, I am impressed by their ability to listen to, and not judge, others. Some of that may simply be their personality, but I suspect some of it also has to do with age, with the wisdom that comes from having seen more of the world than I have yet. The older I get, the more I realize just how hard we struggle, particularly in our younger years. As I age, I am more and more aware of the futility of trying to control my world, though that rarely seems to stop me from trying. Watching the older women in our group care for and nurture those of us who are still struggling to let God have the reins gives me hope that perhaps I will yet develop some of their quiet strength as I continue to move closer to God.

By the end of our first evening together it was clear that we had diverse prayer lives, that each woman had found some very particular ways that connected her with God most fully. We had an abundance of spiritual knowledge, practice, and experience in the room. So we decided to share what we each knew and had experienced, the different disciplines and practices we'd each found meaningful, alternating the leadership each time we met. Experiencing new prayer practices or seeing them from another person's perspective has become an important aspect of our time together. Having a place to talk about our prayer lives, about our lives in general, offering one another prayerful support and encouragement, and praying for one another's concerns, is another.

We agreed to try to meet every two weeks or so, varying the location of the meeting among the homes of those in the group. The host for the evening is in charge of structuring the evening, giving each woman a chance to share some of the things she has found powerful in her own spiritual life. Over the time we have been meeting, we have been exposed to a variety of experiences: Orthodox evening vespers (prayers), praying the rosary, Quaker prayer, guided meditation, reading the Psalms, a Taizé service, a service of healing, and others. We sometimes gather in silence or exchange only brief greetings, and then we let ourselves be led in the prayer practice of the evening. Afterward, we pour some tea, munch a few cookies, and share the joys and sorrows in our lives or in the lives of those we care about deeply. We often close the evening by praying over the concerns mentioned, by reciting a prayer we all know, like the Lord's Prayer, or by sharing a few moments of silence together.

If anyone had told me, even a few years ago, that I would be found learning and praying the rosary one day, I would have been quite surprised. But praying the rosary and lots of other new prayer experiences have come my way since I joined a prayer group.

We had been told by Robin, one of our group members, that she would lead the next meeting and teach us all the rosary. I'm not sure what I expected. I'd never given the rosary much thought, other than selling a book or two on it at the store. I'd seen the strings of beads that are used to pray the rosary, but I had no idea how it was done or why people would do it. Prior to Robin's announcement, I'd assumed it was a "Catholic thing," and, not being Catholic, I gave it no further thought.

Part of the power of the evening was the space that Robin designed for our prayer that night. It was an evening early in the summer, and the living room was lit only by the summer's light. When we gathered that evening, Robin had placed a large metal cross on the coffee table in the center of the circle of chairs where we sat. At each of the four ends of the metal cross was a cut-out circle and four large glasses, each with a lit candle inside. The glasses held the cross up off the table several inches. Around the cross, on the table, were lots of small votive candles, unlit. As we entered, Robin handed us the rosaries she had brought, and we gathered silently around the table until all were present.

When we were all quiet and centered, Robin handed us a sheet of prayers that we would use in saying the rosary and told us a little about how it was done. The rosary itself is a series of fifty beads, divided into five sections called decades. The decades meet at a small metal, and then there is a separate strand of five beads and a crucifix that flow from the metal. There are prayers for each of these items on the rosary.[1]

Robin began the prayers with us, as about half of our group learned to pray the rosary for the first time. Many of the prayers are ones heard in churches on Sunday mornings: the Our Father, the Apostles' Creed, and the Gloria. Beginning with the crucifix, the various prayers are prayed until you reach the metal. Between the metal and the first decade of beads, Scripture or other passages (called the Mysteries) are read. At this point, Robin asked us to pause for a moment and speak aloud or silently of the concerns or joys of our own or of others that we wished the group to hold in prayer. As we named those we wanted to hold in prayer, we lit votive candles and placed them on the metal cross.

For me, learning to pray my prayer requests out loud in the prayer group has been one of the harder things to do. I did not grow up with the tradition of speaking prayers out loud, unless it was in an institutional

1. A good introductory book on the rosary is Basil Pennington, *Praying by Hand* (New York: HarperCollins, 1991).

setting, and the prayers were ones written down and prescribed for us to say. We said those prayers as a group, together, and rarely were any prayers stated individually. Whenever I am asked to speak prayer requests out loud within a group setting, my hands sweat a little, my throat clenches, and my heart races. I'm learning, little by little, to be more comfortable with the process, but it has been a struggle for me.

After hearing everyone's prayer requests we prayed the first decade of the rosary. While moving through each of the ten beads in the decade, the same prayer, the Hail Mary, is repeated while holding each bead: "Hail, Mary, full of grace. The Lord is with you. Blessed are you among women, and blessed is the fruit of your womb, Jesus. Holy Mary, Mother of God, pray for us sinners now and at the hour of our death. Amen."

To read that prayer through quickly may not strike any deep chord within you. It certainly did not with me at first. But praying it over and over again, in a meditative state, opened the prayer up for me in surprising ways. As the prayer was repeated I heard different parts of it each time. "Hail, Mary, full of grace," would make itself heard one time, while on another repetition, I would hear most powerfully the phrase, "the Lord is with you." My understanding and sense of each phrase in the prayer deepened the more often I said it.

I also heard the feminist overtones of the prayer. I am not much of a fan of the goddess theologies that are popular in some feminist circles these days. Praying to a female God makes as little sense as praying to a male God to me; God, to me, is neither male nor female. Nonetheless, I experienced tremendous power through the affirmation of the feminine that evening. Mary, a female, is full of grace. Christianity has not always thought that women could be full of grace. Not only is Mary full of grace, but God is with her. After all the images of men who are full of grace and with whom God dwells, it was good to hear the affirmation that God dwells within women too. The fruit of her womb is also blessed, again, a nice counterpoint to the fact that women and their wombs have not been considered blessed in most of Christian history.

Finally, we prayed to Mary, albeit a saint in some traditions, but a woman who walked this earth, and we asked her to pray for us now and at our deaths. For me, this spoke of the power invoked whenever we ask others to pray for us, or when we pray for others in our world. There is something very comforting in humbly asking Mary, the quintessential mother in many ways, for her prayers. I felt the power of being held by a holy mother who would pray for me always.

As we spoke the prayer over and over, fifty times before we were done, the radical nature of the prayer and my own pleasure at holding up a feminine image of divinity overwhelmed me. For the first time that evening, I was moved by images of a woman blessed by God, dwelling with God, who "mothered" us all with her prayers.

The prayers also helped me to find deep meditative places that evening. The "Hail Mary" prayer functioned for me much as a mantra does in Eastern traditions. Once I had memorized the prayer, I moved further and deeper inward as I continued to recite the words. Repeating the prayer over and over, with others who were doing the same that evening, I had the sense of leaving behind the cares of my day and week and moving into a place of deep connection with God and the others in my group. As we prayed, I was able to hear God's voice, and the concerns and joys of the women in my group, with increasing clarity. And I felt increasing joy to be a part of a group deliberately holding itself in front of God, seeking to align itself with God's way.

As we completed each decade, we stopped to hear Robin read us another of the mysteries. She read the Healing Mysteries to us that evening, five different Gospel stories of Jesus healing the sick. Our prayer requests, likewise, focused on healing. At the beginning, we mostly asked for healing for those we knew well: ourselves, others in our prayer group, friends and family. As the decades continued and our prayerful states deepened, our prayer requests reached more widely out into the world. Not only did we ask for prayers for those we knew, but for those in the world who were living with famine, war, violence, and other atrocities. We sat quietly, in between each decade, speaking our own prayer requests and listening to those of others in the room, and the presence of God was almost palpable. As we lit candles for each request, the otherwise unlit room became alight with our prayerful entreaties.

The rosary ended with a prayer called the Salve Regina, a magnificent prayer that expressed our hopefulness and expectancy: "Hail, holy Queen, Mother of Mercy, our life, our sweetness, and our hope. To you do we cry, poor banished children of Eve. To you do we send up our sighs, mourning, and weeping in this valley of tears. Turn, then, most gracious Advocate, your eyes of mercy toward us. And after this, our exile, show unto us the blessed Fruit of your womb, Jesus. O clement, O loving, O sweet Virgin Mary."

For me, this was one of the most powerful evenings I spent with the prayer group. This is the kind of prayer I would probably not have learned in church, as Protestant churches usually do not pray the rosary. But I found it a rich and meditative experience. Saying the Hail Mary repeatedly, until it became a memorized prayer that almost spoke itself, in a room full of others who are doing the same thing, asking for prayers of healing for our world over the hour it took to say our rosary, touched me deeply. So deeply, in fact, that I have since bought a rosary and continue to use this age-old prayer tradition when I want a period of long contemplative prayer.

Prayer groups are enjoying increasing popularity again these days. Sometimes also called spiritual formation groups, they provide participants with four important things. For many people, they provide a much-needed sense of community. Our culture's focus on the individual, the pace and often transitory nature of our work lives, and even the design of our urban spaces, leave many people with little sense of belonging. Small prayer groups can help to provide the small, intimate community that many of us find lacking in today's world.

Prayer groups can also help people bring balance into their lives by giving their spiritual lives the kind of attention that they often try to give to diet and exercise. They can help move our spiritual lives closer to the top of our busy "to-do" lists.

These small groups can teach knowledge of spiritual practices that might not be taught in other places and times. For a variety of reasons, many churches cannot or do not introduce parishioners to the many spiritual disciplines that are part of the Christian heritage. In today's world, many people have looked to the Eastern traditions for training in meditation and other prayer forms, not knowing that Western religions have held these practices dear through the ages as well. Small groups that lend themselves to caring support and conversation can be good places to learn the various disciplines rooted in Christian tradition.

Lastly, prayer groups provide support and encouragement for our prayer lives, along with a certain level of accountability. As is true in any new practice in our lives, it is hard to develop new habits. Beginning, and continuing to practice, prayer disciplines is no different. Having a regularly scheduled group to help keep your enthusiasm and commitment high can be enormously helpful.

Putting a prayer group together can be as simple as the procedure described for my own prayer group.[2] It is my observation that there are lots of people in our communities who are starved for a place of support and encouragement provided in small prayer groups. You might be surprised at how many of your friends, or friends of friends, will want to join a prayer group you are forming.

Membership in the group can be determined in a number of ways. The group can be open to anyone who wishes to join, as is most often the case within an institutional setting. The advantage to this can be the diversity of people attracted to the group. Groups can also be closed groups, where the members are invited. In some ways, that may screen out diversity, though it doesn't have to. It can also help to insure, though never

---

2. See p. 163 below for some books that provide valuable information about forming and maintaining small groups for prayer.

guarantee, that a more compatible group is formed. Groups can be as small as two people, and can probably grow up to eight or ten, before they grow too large for the kind of intimacy required. Whether your group begins as an open or closed group, you might consider keeping it closed to new members once it has begun, if intimate conversation is part of your agenda. Allowing new people to come and go as the group continues often stifles close or confidential conversations.

If the leader of the group has not predetermined the schedule and structure of the meeting times, that should be explored and agreed upon during the first meeting. Based on the goals and desires of the group, you might choose to meet weekly, twice a month, monthly, or at some other interval. Generally, however, the less often you meet, the harder it is to have a sense of group identity. You might also discuss commitment to the group. You may or may not need to set detailed rules about attendance, but for the sake of continuity and support, all members of the group need to be committed to being at as many of the meetings as possible.

Choose to meet in a place that is conducive to your prayer pursuits. Having a group of ten people meet in a large sanctuary of a church, for instance, can feel very uncomfortable. Meeting in a small chapel or someone's living room may feel more intimate and private. Also plan to spend time at your first meeting determining how you will structure the meetings. It is not at all essential that each meeting have the same overall structure, but it may be helpful to have some common elements from meeting to meeting that everyone understands, which bind the meetings together and forge group identity.

Finally, form the group around a particular goal or concept. Perhaps that will be the desire to learn a particular type of prayer, such as contemplative prayer. Another possibility is to form a reading group that focuses on a book of spiritual nurture. Or it can be, as it was for us, to provide a supportive environment for learning more about all sorts of prayer and for encouragement and support in our prayer lives. Others form groups around the prayer requests of people they know or hear about and meet regularly to update the lists, to report on the individuals asking for prayer, and to pray together. Whatever your goal, it is important for everyone to be clear about it from the start.

☙

If you are just beginning to discover, or rediscover, Christian spirituality, starting a prayer group of your own may seem an overwhelming task. That is particularly true if you've been outside of Christian community for a number of years. A variety of churches these days, however, are forming small groups within the parish, and you might well find one of these groups a hospitable place to explore prayer within the Christian context and community, even if you are not interested in becoming a church member at this time.

A friend of mine, Lucy, began a small prayer group in her church a couple of years ago that has since expanded to include members of four local parishes, but her group is a good model of what you might expect from a small-group experience in the church. Lucy is ordained in the Episcopal Church and began her group, one that says the rosary weekly, at her parish one year during Advent (a period of about a month before Christmas). It began by meeting in the chapel, but that space felt too large for the small group of ten members, and it has since moved to her home. By group consensus, she prepares the space and the Mysteries that will be read each week, which allows the members of the group to just come and participate. This is often one of the great advantages of joining a church or other group led by a particular leader. Those of us with busy schedules sometimes need a place to simply come and participate, without having additional preparation and work responsibilities.

Over time, the group has changed and grown in some important ways, as all healthy groups do. In the beginning, the mysteries that were read came from the Saint Augustine Prayer Book, an older book with traditional language. The group has moved from that to a book of feminist meditations for the rosary, appreciated by all the members of the group, even the one male participant. At the beginning of their time together, however, several of the group members disliked inclusive language — language that tries to avoid references to gender when gender is not clear and avoids using male words for groups that include males and females. Over time, and without any conscious effort or conversation, the group embraced the inclusive language. Prayer groups change us, if we let them, by exposing us to new experiences and to the perspectives of others.

Lucy's group has also survived what any group must if it is to stay together for any period of time. As with any relationship, groups go through an initial cycle of infatuation with the group, before individual personalities, problems, or arguments begin to surface. A group's success often depends on being able to name the difficulties when they do arise and to discuss them openly. Within Lucy's group some hostility developed between several members over an issue outside of the rosary group. While everyone continued to attend the prayer group, the hostility was felt by all. It was the group's ability to name and discuss the anger and its effect on the group that has allowed them to move past the problem and continue to pray together. To be a member of a small group that hopes to stay together is to accept the responsibility for honest communication, whether it be about joys or hurts. Just as honesty is important, so is confidentiality. Small prayer groups are most effective when members know they can trust one another and that their words will not be repeated outside of the group, that they are free to speak openly.

❧

Honesty, trust, and commitment to a prayer group does not happen overnight for group members, but when it does happen, the rewards are tremendous. By talking about God's movement in your own life to others, you often discover directions and understandings that eluded you previously. And perhaps the greatest reward is that, as a member of the group, you will be the instrument through which God speaks to someone else in the group.

About five or six months after our prayer group began meeting, Andrea and her husband experienced a sudden and unexpected loss of a close family friend. Their pain was deep, and all of the members of our prayer group felt it keenly. The friend's funeral was held some distance away from where we all live, so we could not be with Andrea to support her at that particular time. But we could offer our own prayers for her healing at our next prayer group meeting. Andrea accepted our invitation to be the focus of a healing service, and at her request we invited her husband to be present as well.

In a moment of utter concern for Andrea, I offered to prepare the service for the evening. It was only later, when I realized that I'd never done such a thing, that I felt a bit of panic! Nonetheless, I sat down with a variety of prayer books several days before the service, hoping that something meaningful would come together. Over the next couple of hours, I poured through the books, looking for prayers and biblical passages that could speak to the pain and suffering of my friends. In many ways, it was the most prayerful two hours I'd spent in ages. I felt as if I was guided to just the right words, the right actions for each part of the service. I heard no voices booming out of the skies or even voices in my own mind, but I was guided nonetheless, and a couple of hours later an entire service of healing was typed on my computer screen. Though the service was God's gift to Andrea and her husband, I felt gifted too. My wish to create something meaningful opened me to God's presence and guidance in a way I've rarely experienced.

We met the following week for the service of healing for an evening that touched us all deeply. The service lasted about an hour and a half and was filled with tears, and even some laughter, as Andrea and Bill recounted stories of their friend's gifts to their lives. We prayed for God's healing presence to be with them. We read of God's promises for eternal life from the Bible. We laid our hands on Andrea and Bill, invoked God's assurance and guidance during this sad time, and sang hymns of hopefulness. Throughout it all we cried and we laughed, and as best as we were able we joined with

God in healing and encouraging Andrea and Bill. It was an extraordinary evening, and one that would probably not have been possible without the many months of trusted, intimate conversations that came before. It was a night when God shone clearly through one and all, when we were reminded that God lives in and speaks through each one of us when we let that happen.

It is experiences like that, and like the evening with the rosary, that keep me strongly committed to the prayer group. My schedule is often hectic, and there have been many evenings when I haven't felt like going back out in the evening. I also have a tendency, sometimes, to prefer being alone in my prayers, to hole up with God by myself. But I am reminded in my prayer group how often God speaks through the people around me. My relationship with those with whom I share my prayer life is now a steadfast part of my romance with God.

– S I X –

Spiritual Reading

I remember very clearly the day I first realized that I had stumbled on some version of sacred or meditative reading. I was sitting in bed on a dreary winter day with a manuscript in my lap. The pages were from a forthcoming book by Frederick Buechner, one of my favorite Christian writers. Though I was reading the book in order to review it for my store's newsletter, I suddenly realized that I was reading intently, that I was dialoguing with the book and with God as I read. It was as if I were praying the words on the page rather than reading them. My definition of prayer expanded that day and now includes the reading that I do for my soul and to increase my understanding of and connection to God.

Spiritual reading, formally known as *lectio divina* in Christian circles, involves reading less for intellectual stimulation or knowledge than for a deeper understanding of how the text might convey God's word for you at this particular time. And, like any other spiritual discipline, it is also a gift of time and attention that we give to God. In *lectio divina* how much you read matters less than how deeply and prayerfully you read. Those who practice *lectio* regularly, for instance, might read a whole page of Scripture or some other book in a given day, or they might read only a couple of sentences, or even just a few words. The point of the discipline is to read slowly, with great mindfulness, and to stop when a word or phrase catches your attention. Staying with that word or phrase, repeating it silently or aloud, meditating on it, letting it rest in your heart and soul, can be a powerful way of communicating with God and allowing God to communicate with you.

For those of us who read a lot professionally, *lectio divina* may never be the way we spend our time connecting with God. *Lectio divina* requires us to read in a leisurely way. For me, the habit of reading or, more often, skimming through texts rapidly to get the sense of them, is so deeply ingrained that sacred reading sometimes happens more by accident than by design. During retreat times, however, when I have time to slow down and do things differently, *lectio divina* can become a place of deep connection to God for me.

On one such retreat, I was given the "dry bones" passage to read from Ezekiel 37. Ezekiel is one of the prophets of the Hebrew Scriptures who speaks to the

Israelites in their exile, assuring them of the Lord's presence with them. The passage recalls the prophet's time in a valley, one that is littered with dry bones. God asks Ezekiel if the bones can live again, and Ezekiel responds that only God can answer that question. God then commands Ezekiel to prophesy to the bones, to tell them to listen to the word of God and live again. Ezekiel does as God asks, and to the bones are added sinews, flesh, skin, and finally breath. The dry bones live again. God tells Ezekiel that the dry bones were like the house of Israel, dried up and lost, but capable of being brought back to life. The passage closes with God's promise:

> [12] Therefore prophesy, and say to them, Thus says the LORD God: I am going to open your graves, and bring you up from your graves, O my people; and I will bring you back to the land of Israel. [13] And you shall know that I am the LORD, when I open your graves, and bring you up from your graves, O my people. [14] I will put my spirit within you, and you shall live, and I will place you on your own soil; then you shall know that I, the LORD, have spoken and will act, says the LORD.

What we normally hear in this passage, and what is often preached in churches, is that our own dry bones, our old and dead ways or our periods of spiritual dryness, can and will be revived by the word of God. True enough. But the point of *lectio* is to move further into the text than we would otherwise. Though we may have heard a passage many times before in our lives, by paying careful attention we allow new understandings to surprise us. What caught my attention when I read the passage slowly was the promise made in verse 14: "I will put my spirit within you, and you shall live, and I will place you on your own soil." The words, "I will place you on your own soil," stopped me cold. They might as well have been in neon in front of me, and I could read no further. I put my Bible aside and let the words fill my heart and mind.

The words rang like an incredibly wonderful promise in my mind. At the same time, I wondered: Where am I now, if not on my own soil? What would be the kind of place that God considered to be the soil that suited me perfectly? From my experiences as a backyard gardener, I know that I can increase or decrease a plant's chances of living, and even thriving, by where I plant it and how I tend to it. One year, I planted zucchini in a spot that I thought would be sunny enough, but I was wrong. The plant itself grew, but each time an actual zucchini appeared, it grew about an inch long, and then rotted and died. I had planted it in a spot rich enough to sustain basic life, but not rich enough to bear fruit.

I have also planted myself, sometimes, in places where I cannot grow. I accepted a job once that I was ill-suited for, and by the end of the first week, I knew that I would not thrive in that job. Nevertheless,

I stayed in the job for a year and a half before taking another job. It was one of the most miserable times of my life and affected not only my feelings about work, but about life in general. I came away from the job feeling like a failure, and it was many months before I felt confident about my work and abilities again.

But now, in this text from Ezekiel, I heard God promising me that I would be placed someplace especially suited to me, a place where I could grow and thrive, a place that God selected specifically for me. I wondered how I would know when that had happened. Perhaps it has happened already, and I have been planted in my own soil and I'm just not aware of that. Or perhaps I am part of the way to that place of homecoming, that place where I will grow and thrive, and now I need to listen carefully for God's word to take me the rest of the way there. I was reminded to listen carefully for God's guidance in career choices, in my spiritual life, and in my world as a whole.

I found myself wondering, too, why God would take such extraordinary care, finding just the right place to plant *me*. Certainly, I have done nothing that would earn me such honor. God's promise in Ezekiel comes without strings, however. God can and will, finally, plant me where I belong. That promise gives me hope, strength, and courage.

At some point, when all of these thoughts had finished pouring through me, I lapsed into a deep and quiet period of meditation, a time of just resting in the knowledge of the promise given in Ezekiel — a quiet time in which the emotions of gratitude and great joy rose to the surface and left me, briefly, in gentle tears. I ended my time with a prayer of thankfulness to God for the promise given.

Lectio divina has its origins in the early centuries of Christian history, but is best known for its widespread use by St. Benedict in the fourth and fifth centuries. Benedict began several religious communities, governed by what is known as the Rule of St. Benedict, which was (and is) a guide to daily life in Benedictine communities. In it, Benedict instructed the monks to give the best time of the day to sacred reading, and large parts of the monks' days, and even the whole day on Sunday, were devoted to *lectio divina.*

Benedict did not specify, however, an exact procedure for this sacred reading, and so there are almost as many ways to structure a regular practice of *lectio divina* as there are individuals who practice the discipline. Almost every book or article you can read on the subject suggests a slightly different sequence of events, and finally, each of us must structure our practice in the way that is most helpful for us. There are some basic elements, however, that are common to most understandings of sacred reading. In Latin, the four basic elements are

known as *lectio, meditatio, oratio,* and *contemplatio.*
Adding the letter "n" to the end of each word gives
you the basic English equivalent: lection, meditation,
oration, and contemplation.

Lectio, or lection, means reading. Many churches
structure their readings for Sunday morning worship,
and other days, around an established lectionary, or
cycle of readings from the Bible. Consequently, some
people use the lectionary as the source of their reading for each day. Others pick a particular book of the
Bible and read slowly through the book each day until a particular phrase or word catches their attention.
A variety of other books can be used in *lectio divina*
too. Traditionally people have read biographies or autobiographies of saints and other holy people or any other
book which has a spiritual focus.

In sacred reading we read slowly and attentively.
Reading aloud, even in a small whisper, can often help
you to read more slowly and helps you to hear the
words you are reading more deeply. When reading, pay
attention to any words or phrases that grab your attention. You can even repeat them over and over if you
wish. Using the word or phrase, you can move on to
your meditation time whenever you are ready.

Meditatio, or meditation, is the time to let the word
or phrase speak more deeply to you. You can do that in
a variety of ways. Some people place themselves within
the passage, assuming one of the characters' parts and

imagining the story unfolding around them, fleshing out the text. Others imagine that God is speaking the words directly to them, and listen for what the words have to say about their lives here and now. Some people, if using a biblical text, take out a biblical commentary and read a little about the historical or sociological context of the passage in order to understand it better before interpreting the passage's meaning for their own life. There are no right or wrong ways to spend meditation time; it will vary according to each individual's own best ways of praying.

Oratio, or oration in English, is the part of sacred reading in which we offer a prayer to God and this, too, will take a variety of different forms. This prayer is a response to what has been revealed in the reading and the meditation or study you have done up to now. It can be done in writing, using a journal to write your response to God's words in your life. Other people speak their prayers, aloud or silently. Still others may dance a prayer to God, or make their response in some other creative way. That response might include a wide variety of feelings: gratitude, sorrow, anger, hurt, and any other emotion which the reading has tapped.

Finally, in the process we fall into a more quiet contemplation. When we have thought through the passage and when we have given our response to God, we rest quietly with God and our new understandings of God's words in our lives. It is a time of sitting quietly, letting the insights and prayers of the previous time rest in our hearts, of letting them take shape, perhaps as we would let a loaf of bread rise. Letting the insights and prayers of the previous period have some time to find a place to live in our hearts and minds will help them remain with us firmly.

This whole process can take fifteen minutes or it can last an hour or more, according to individual preferences. There is nothing wrong with beginning your practice with fifteen-minute time segments, which is probably the shortest time period for actually completing the process. As you continue and deepen your practice, it is likely that you will find yourself giving the process more time.

There is, of course, nothing set in stone in this process. Macrina Wiederkehr, for instance, in her wonderful book *The Song of the Seed,* suggests a different sequence of events.[1] She suggests we do *lectio divina,* which she calls "romancing the word," in the morning, beginning the time with a period of quieting, moving on to reading, and then returning to quiet again, without trying to contemplate the text. Then she moves on to actual meditation on the text and from there to prayer in response to the words. Finally, she recommends that we take a few moments at the end of the day to review how that morning's reading has influenced our day and

1. Macrina Wiederkehr, *The Song of the Seed: A Monastic Way of Tending the Soul* (New York: HarperCollins, 1995).

record those thoughts in a journal. I have used Wieder-kehr's suggested way of sacred reading while on silent retreat and have been amazed at the power of the text to shape my perception of what happens to me during the day. The morning's text often stayed with me throughout the entire day, coming to me periodically in relation to something happening around or inside me. At day's end, when I would reflect on it consciously again, my understanding of the text was often deeper and clearer.

A friend of mine, Janet, began doing sacred reading about five years ago. For quite some time, she did it every morning, no matter what. These days she is gentler with herself, and does it as often as she needs, which means that she does it often at times, and less often at others. But she has been consistent enough with her practice for the last five years that she finds it an indispensable part of her spiritual life today.

Janet is a morning person. She rises around 5:00 a.m. most mornings, while her husband is still asleep and the house is quiet. When she chooses to do her reading, she makes herself a cup of coffee and settles into the area she has set up for her reading. She calls it her "quiet time."

This kind of quiet time began for Janet when she was asked to take on the leadership of a large volunteer project. Many people thought she was competent to do the work, but Janet found it intimidating and worried that she wasn't up to the task. She decided that if she were going to do the project, she was going to need help from God, and that help could be found in some quiet time alone with God each morning. Her mother had always read from a booklet produced by her church that included the day's assigned lections (passages from the Bible), followed by an interpretive paragraph applying the reading to our daily lives. Janet had read from this same booklet off and on during her life as well. At this point, however, it became the constant companion of her morning quiet time.

Making herself quiet and comfortable, Janet lights a candle and reads the assigned Bible passage for the day. She has been a reader of the Bible her whole life and has marked each passage every time she reads it, sometimes adding the date. So her Bible is full of small pencil marks where she has read before, with some passages being marked many, many times. Even with her life-long knowledge of many of the Bible's passages, however, she finds new meaning as she reads more deeply or from a different perspective, according to her mood or the events of recent days.

The reading is followed by a period of response to the passage that can include meditation, journaling, and even drawing. Some days she finds herself drawing pictures of the images in the passage, trying to understand what the words look like in physical reality. Other days she finds herself writing about the events in her world, sometimes related to the passage at hand, and sometimes not. This quiet time in the morning, however, helps set the tone for the rest of her day. Janet often finds the passages coming back to her, not only throughout that day, but for many days or weeks afterward. After many years of practicing this way, she has learned to become quiet much more quickly, and can't imagine doing without her "quiet time" for long.

It was, in fact, through her quiet time, that Janet realized she had a drinking problem. Though few who knew her would have thought she had trouble with drinking, Janet knew that she drank many drinks each evening in order to block out the various pains of her life. The drink helped her numb and ignore them. The quiet time, however, brought the problem into focus for her. "When I was quiet with my very own thoughts, and with my journal, and with my morning reading, I was no longer able to pretend that everything was fine," says Janet today.

This didn't happen immediately, but built up over a period of years. As Janet looks back at her journals today, she sees how unhappy she was and how much of that she put into her reading and journaling. Janet also found herself changing and growing during this time. "You cannot read the word of God every morning and not be changed," she says with deep conviction.

One morning, during her quiet time, she prayed to God: "You know how miserable I am, and I know that this drinking is way out of hand. And I'm willing, no matter what it takes, to stop drinking." She didn't stop drinking that day, or even for many months after that, but the prayer that she'd spoken to God stayed with her, in the back of her mind. Another family crisis prompted Janet to finally stop drinking. She quit one night three years ago, and has not had a drink since. The quiet time, along with Alcoholics Anonymous and the church, helps Janet maintain her sobriety.

When Janet began her reading years ago, a friend who was a priest and psychologist told her that the practice of reading and quiet contemplation and journaling would make all the difference in the world to her in a few years' time. That statement alone is one of the things that kept Janet resolute in making space for her quiet time most days. Now, many years later, she finds that her friend's statement was true. She finds that she is able to be quiet much more quickly and deeply than she could years ago. She also finds that she reads more critically. At the beginning she read the Bible passages and a short interpretation of them and thought that the commentary was, of course, the definitive interpretation of the text. Today, she reads critically, arguing with parts of the text and the meaning of it, and that enriches her life. She used to think that only experts could interpret the Bible, and she has learned otherwise.

Her reading has also convinced her of the power of words in general. Words set up our expectations and our hopes, and so Janet has learned to pay more attention to her own words, to herself, and to others. And, finally, Janet has found that the reading and quiet time have allowed her to be more of herself. She feels less need to assume roles that society sometimes assigns to us and enjoys her life more. The quiet time is not the only factor in the changes in her life, but it is an important element, and one she cannot do without.

Janet's story illustrates some of the things that are important to consider when doing *lectio divina*. First is finding a place and time that is free of distraction. If you already have a prayer corner or a place set up in your home where you go to pray, that is a good place for *lectio* as well. There is nothing that says you must use the same place every time you do sacred reading, but having one place where you do it can often be a help. Over time, your body begins to know instinctively that every time you return to your prayer corner it is sacred time, and that may make it easier to quiet yourself for prayer. Whether or not you have a particular spot for your reading, try to find a place that is free of distractions, such as phone calls, visitors, or other disturbances.

Choose what you will read in advance of beginning

your reading time. There are any number of choices for reading material. Some of the most popular are:

1. You can pick one book of the Bible and read through it sequentially over a period of time — whatever it takes. If you are going to read from the Bible, reading through an entire book allows your reading to remain in context. This means that you are not trying to guess what is happening in the text, or who is speaking to whom, and so on. This can be particularly useful if you are new to reading the Bible and do not know many of the stories contained in it.

2. You can also follow the lectionary readings of the Catholic Church, or one of the Protestant or ecumenical lectionaries. The lectionary readings, assigned in a two- or three-year cycle, cover the major stories and events in the Bible and will give you a good overview of the text if you continue to read. Generally, there are four readings assigned for each day: one from the Hebrew Scriptures or Old Testament, one from the Psalms, one from the Epistles or letters of the New Testament, and one from the four Gospels (Matthew, Mark, Luke, and John) of the New Testament. For the purposes of *lectio,* where we are reading a small amount of text for deeper understanding, you may want to pick just one of the lections to read each day.

3. Various books, most notably Wiederkehr's *Song of the Seed* and Thelma Hall's *Too Deep for Words*,[2] include lots of scriptural suggestions for sacred reading. Some, like Wiederkehr's, are organized around themes, such as sowing a seed. Others, like Hall's, categorize the readings under particular emotions.

4. Almost any book that discusses spirituality can be appropriate for sacred reading. The lives of the saints or the writings of the Desert Fathers are classical suggestions for *lectio*. They are helpful for some, while others find them full of patriarchal assumptions, unfamiliar language, and other troubling features. Biographies and autobiographies of holy people can be instructive reading. So can sacred poetry, literature, and many books you would find in the spirituality section of your local bookstore. Various publishers are putting out edited collections of the writings of well-known authors, some of them arranged in short segments for 365 days, and these can be a useful focus for your reading.

But perhaps what Janet's story illustrates best is the power of staying with a particular practice, like *lectio divina*, for a long period. What is true of relationships

---

2. Thelma Hall, *Too Deep for Words: Rediscovering Lectio Divina* (Mahwah, N.J.: Paulist Press, 1988).

is also true of our romance with God. Long-lasting and powerful relationships are not formed overnight. The best and closest ones form over many years and are the result of shared experiences and a deep knowing of one another in all sorts of moods and emotional states. *Lectio divina* presents us with an opportunity to know God, and to be known by God, that is a lot like developing a close relationship. By reading about God, by reading God's words, by responding to them and dialoguing with God about your understandings, over the years you will come to know God better and to feel better known by God.

– S E V E N –

Benediction

"She said what?" That was my first response to the proposal that I write this book. Mike Leach, who would eventually become my editor, cornered me at a professional conference, told me of his idea, and recounted that a mutual friend had suggested that I should be the one to write the book. I couldn't imagine finding time to write a book, nor was I the least convinced that I had anything helpful to say. I told Mike I'd think about it, and left it at that. Over the next couple of days, I talked to him some more about the book, and late one night it began to take shape in my head. By the third day, I knew that I would have to write the book, that it would haunt me forever if I didn't.

What I didn't see at the time was God's hand in the process. One of my spiritual directors, an author herself, promised me that the book would be one of my best spiritual teachers, and she was quite right. In the course of the writing, I have been forced to clarify many of my own thoughts and feelings. I have had struggles with God that rival Jacob's struggle with the angel (Gen. 32:22–32). And I have found places of communion with God that are deeper than I'd ever imagined. My own romance with God, with what is holy, grows daily, and I am most grateful.

It is my hope that this book will also help you begin, or deepen, your own romance with God. People who are beginning their spiritual journey often feel that there are rules or "right ways" to do things, that there are prescribed paths that must be walked. Though it may be true that there are parts of the pathway we must all walk at one time or another, there are lots of good starting places. I do not think that God cares *where* we start our journey, only that we begin somewhere. Wherever you choose to start, may your romance be rich and full of surprises. May it heal you and make you laugh. May it be the love that sustains you when life is dark and that which shines brightly through you on the best of days.

Resources

Spiritual Direction

Guenther, Margaret. *Holy Listening: The Art of Spiritual Direction.* Boston: Cowley Publications, 1992. An extremely readable and helpful introduction to the process of spiritual direction. Written as a book to guide those who are providing spiritual direction, this is nevertheless useful for those seeking direction and gives readers a solid sense of what to expect.

Leech, Kenneth. *Soul Friend: An Invitation to Spiritual Direction.* New York: HarperSanFrancisco, 1980. A more academic treatment of spiritual direction. Particularly useful for its historical overview of the practice of spiritual direction in Christian history.

Thomson, Marjorie J. *Soul Feast: An Invitation to the Christian Spiritual Life.* Louisville: Westminster John Knox Press, 1995. Chapter 7 in this book is a good and brief introduction to spiritual direction, including what to expect and how to pick a spiritual director.

For locating spiritual directors in your area:

Spiritual Directors International
1329 Seventh Avenue
San Francisco, CA 94122
415–566–1560

Center for Christian Spirituality
175 Ninth Avenue
New York, NY 10011
212–675–1524

Retreats

Angell, Jeannette L. *All Ground Is Holy: A Guide to the Christian Retreat.* Harrisburg, Pa.: Morehouse Publishing, 1993. A brief and accessible guide to the beginning retreatant. Includes information on preparation (what to wear, bring), worship on retreats, meeting with a spiritual director, and other practical questions for those new to retreat experiences. The appendix to the book includes names and addresses of various retreat places in seventeen states.

Housden, Roger. *Retreat: Time Apart for Silence and Solitude.* New York: HarperCollins, 1995. A brief and concise description of retreats from various perspectives, including Christianity. Beautiful photographs also make this book pleasing, providing a perspective on retreats that cannot be supplied by words alone.

Joy, Janet. *A Place Apart: Houses of Prayer and Retreat Centers in North America.* Trabuco Canyon, Calif.: Source Books, 1995. A list of retreat centers in the United States, Canada, and a few in places like Mexico, Bermuda, and the West Indies.

Kelly, Jack and Marcia. *Sanctuaries: The Complete United States, A Guide to Lodgings in Monasteries, Abbeys, and Retreats.* New York: Bell Tower, 1996. A listing of hundreds of places across the fifty states that provide retreat lodgings. Of the places listed 127 have information on accommodations, available services, fees, transportation, and hospitality. Hundreds of other places are listed with their addresses and phone numbers for your own review. Includes retreats affiliated with a variety of religions, though primarily Catholic and Episcopalian.

Nouwen, Henri. *Genesee Diary: Report from a Trappist Monastery.* Garden City, N.Y.: Doubleday and Co., 1976. A journal of Nouwen's spiritual journey while living as a monk in a

Trappist monastery for seven months. While most will not have the option of the kind of retreat Nouwen describes, his daily recordings of his spiritual journey and his learning to love the silence and stillness are quite helpful.

Regalbuto, Robert. *A Guide to Monastic Guest Houses.* 2d ed. Harrisburg, Pa.: Morehouse Publishing, 1992. A guide to monastic communities that provide space for those seeking some time apart. Includes locations in thirty-three states and seven Canadian provinces.

Rupp, Joyce. *May I Have This Dance?* Notre Dame, Ind.: Ave Maria Press, 1992. Suggestions for twelve retreats, either for individuals or groups, prepared according to the twelve months. Rupp provides a scriptural focus for each retreat, a short meditation of her own, and some suggestions for prayers, rituals, and exercises that might focus the retreatant. A very helpful guide for those wanting to plan retreats for themselves, a small group of friends, or a large church group.

Zaleski, Philip. *The Recollected Heart.* New York: HarperCollins, 1995. An accessible resource for people who are thinking of going on a silent retreat, or for those who want to plan their own retreat. Zaleski's book provides lots of detail about preparation and actually conducting a three-day retreat on your own.

Organizations to contact for information on a variety of retreat centers:

Retreats International
PO Box 1067
Notre Dame, IN 46556
219–631–5320

Institute for Spiritual Leadership
4906 S. Greenwood Avenue
Chicago, IL 60615

The following retreat centers offer programs at various times during the year. Many are one-week retreats focused on a topic or discipline. Write to be placed on their mailing lists:

Holden Village (Lutheran)
Chelan, WA 98816
(no telephone lines in Holden Village)

Ghost Ranch Conference Center (Presbyterian)
H.C. 77 – Box 11
Abiquiu, NM 87510
800–821–5145
505–685–4333

Kirkridge
Bangor, PA 18013 610–588–1793

Spirituality Online

This area is so new that there are few book resources to guide you. If you are already familiar with the World Wide Web and the Internet, you will find many Christian spirituality sites by using the search tools available from your service provider. If you would like some suggested starting places, try the following book:

Kellner, Mark A. *God on the Internet: Your Complete Guide to Enhancing Your Spiritual Life via the Internet and Online Services.* Foster City, Calif.: IDG Books, 1996. Kellner's book provides readers of all faiths lots of good starting places on the Internet and World Wide Web. Many of the sites he recommends lead to a variety of other sites and will help new seekers get their bearings.

If you are interested in exploring the Ecunet computer network, you can get information on it by calling 1–800–RE-ECUNET.

Prayer Groups

I recommend these two books with the caution that both are written assuming that groups will happen in churches and that both have a somewhat conservative approach to prayer groups. Nonetheless, both have helpful information about forming and maintaining small groups, whether they are within the church or not.

Arnold, Jeffrey. *The Big Book on Small Groups.* Downers Grove, Ill.: InterVarsity Press, 1992. Full of information about forming small groups and the leadership skills required to keep them afloat. Good ideas on forming and maintaining community.

Smith, James Bryan. *A Spiritual Formation Workbook: Small Group Resources for Nurturing Christian Growth.* San Francisco: HarperSanFrancisco, 1991. Includes a chapter on starting groups, as well as a series of Bible studies that might be used for group discussion.

Spiritual Reading

Mass, Robin, and Gabriel O'Donnell, O.P. *Spiritual Traditions for the Contemporary Church.* Nashville: Abingdon Press, 1990. A brief practicum following chapter 1 of this book provides an overview of *lectio divina* (sacred reading), as well as suggested exercises for using it as an individual or in group situations.

Michael, Chester P., and Marie C. Norrisey. *Prayer and Temperament: Different Prayer Forms for Different Personality Types.* Charlottesville, Va.: The Open Door, Inc., 1991. *Lectio divina* is the subject of chapter 3 of this book, providing a succinct overview of the subject, particularly in light of the Myers Briggs Personality Indicator. The information in the chapter is useful whether or not you are familiar with Myers Briggs.

Thompson, Marjorie J. *Soul Feast: An Invitation to the Christian Spiritual Life.* Louisville: Westminster John Knox Press, 1995. Chapter 2 of this book looks at spiritual reading and makes suggestions for newcomers who want to learn the practice. Of particular use are the suggestions about authors and texts that might make good reading for *lectio divina*.

Vest, Norvene. *No Moment Too Small: Rhythms of Silence, Prayer, and Holy Reading*. Kalamazoo, Mich.: Cistercian Publications, and Boston: Cowley Publications, 1994. Vest looks at the Benedictine way of life as a whole in this short book, but pays particular attention to *lectio divina* in chapter 2. After examining the history and method of *lectio divina,* she provides four different exercises that will help novices explore the practice.

Wiederkehr, Macrina. *The Song of the Seed: A Monastic Way of Tending the Soul*. New York: HarperCollins, 1995. Wiederkehr's gentle voice in this book provides excellent guidance to those new to *lectio divina*. The first two chapters explain the process, and the remaining chapters provide suggestions for thirty days of reading, along with a suggested focus, prayers, and questions that go with each text. Can be used by individuals or groups.